JOHN DEMJANJUK
The Real Story

JOHN DEMJANJUK

The Real Story

Jim McDonald

Amana Books
Brattleboro, VT

Table of Contents

INTRODUCTION

This book is the result of my involvement in the John Demjanjuk case, a travesty of justice also touted as the "Ivan the Terrible" case which culminated in what has been described in Israel as the Trial of the Century and which has resulted in a controversial death sentence. My participation came about because earlier refugee work had brought me into contact with the late U.S. Displaced Persons Commissioner Edward Mark O'Connor, recognized at the time as the world's foremost expert on refugees and human migration. Our friendship and consultations continued long after the termination of the DP Program. O'Connor's son, Mark, an attorney interested in refugees in his own right, and I were, naturally, acquainted. Mark knew of my professional background, was aware that I understood the European "mentality," and knew that I was a skilled interrogator. After Mark had been retained by John Demjanjuk's family to defend him, he informed me that he had been declared persona non grata in Poland and, since most of the key witnesses and evidence were in that country, he needed assistance in gathering evidence there. He asked if I would be interested and I readily accepted the offer, having become intrigued by the many bewildering elements of the case which Mark had described to me. Thus, I became Mark O'Connor's principal investigator in the John Demjanjuk case.

Although it has been a great privilege for me to have played a small role in this case, it has been heartbreaking to have participated in what I and many others perceive to be one of the most rigged, corrupt and fixed trials in history. The apparent suicide on December 1,1988 of Dov Eitan, a retired Israeli judge who had recently joined the Demjanjuk defense team, only serves to heighten the grave suspicions that this case has aroused, and further underlines its overall unsavoriness.

This book could not have been written without the contributions of some twenty well-versed participants and researchers in this case. Since several of them expressed fear of their names being in print, it is my decision not to acknowledge any of the contributors, knowing full well that they will be more than rewarded if John Demjanjuk is eventually given justice.

CHAPTER ONE – BEGINNINGS

John Demjanjuk's alleged crimes took place in eastern Poland in 1942-1943. As information was developed over an approximate ten-year period, Russia became interested in Demjanjuk as a "traitor to the Motherland" because he did not commit suicide instead of allowing himself to be taken prisoner by the German Army during World War II. The Israelis, on the other hand, wanted Demjanjuk under their Nazi and Nazi Collaborator Law as a major participant in the genocide of the Jewish people.

If any country should have been given the option for a trial, had there been valid reasons for it, that country was Poland, the locale of the killings and atrocities at the Treblinka death camp near the Russian border. A second more realistic site for the trial could have been Germany since that country, after all, was the fountainhead of Nazism, and the so-called Government-General of Poland was at that time under its jurisdiction.

It was to Poland, therefore, that I was sent in order to collect more information. Prior to my departure, I had been provided with the name and phone number of a man in Warsaw who supposedly was thoroughly versed on the Demjanjuk matter and might have valuable information. On arrival, I phoned Sigmund Nowak,[1] who sounded extremely fearful and refused to meet with me in my hotel. A subway terminal was being built nearby and we agreed to meet at its entrance that night at a given time. Nowak, a tall slender man with raised collar on his coat, greeted me and we shook hands. He could not speak English; I could not speak Polish; we therefore communicated in German. Although he insisted that John Demjanjuk was not the real "Ivan the Terrible" whom Israel was pursuing, he was unable to provide any concrete evidence that could be used in court. An interesting consequence of this event was that in a matter of days, my name was splashed in the Israeli press to the effect that I was in Poland trying to find "false witnesses" on behalf of John Demjanjuk. I was accused of telling these witnesses what evidence was being sought from them, and that I promised them trips to the United States along with generous financial rewards.

A certain Jacek Wilczur, Chief Specialist of the Central Commission for the Investigation of Nazi Crimes in Poland, was the conduit for these defamatory

---

1. A pseudonym to protect the individual's identity.

accusations that were passed on to the Israelis. Since these false accusations might possibly have a grave influence on the trial, I wondered that the government of Poland was not the subject of a massive lawsuit because of Wilczur's actions. But the Central Commission is part of the Polish judiciary and is admittedly assisting Israel in the Demjanjuk case. It was later learned from various sources that Sigmund Nowak "had agreed to testify against Mr. Demjanjuk."

Two days later Leo Kaz,[2] my interpreter, and I decided to drive to Treblinka and its surrounding villages to seek out residents who were survivors of that camp. After a lengthy drive on rustic roads, we turned into a driveway and saw a long, low building with open front and panels decorated with artistic inscriptions. Several farm-type people were about, and we proceeded to park in a designated zone. One of the people told Leo in Polish that there was a caretaker of Treblinka, which appeared to be a huge memorial park, who would be glad to explain the history of the camp and escort us around the grounds. He pointed out a nearby house and went scurrying to get him.

Tadeusz Kuryluk, also a rustic type with mismatched brown uniform and peaked railroader cap, extended a warm, friendly greeting and shook hands with us. He gave us some statistical data about Treblinka. Its size was over thirteen hectares, one hectare being equal to 2.47 acres. During its infamous use, it was surrounded by a three-meter-high barbed wire fence. The operational staff consisted of several dozen S.S. men and one hundred Fascist assistants, plus fifteen hundred work inmates to supervise the undressing, sorting of clothing, etc. We began to walk on an immense green area that was surrounded by dark green, seemingly impenetrable forests.

After studying two memorial monuments, Kuryluk pointed out a long row of upright stones leading into a wood. These were sites for executions, he explained. Continuing, we saw what appeared to be an endless row of railroad ties apparently made out of stone because they were so perfectly shaped. The superintendent explained that these were a symbol of the real railroad tracks on which the trains ran, bringing in victims from all over Europe to be exterminated. We walked parallel to the tracks for approximately a quarter of a mile, noting a mammoth four-story chimney looming larger as we approached it. This chimney symbolized the death chambers at the end of the "Street to Heaven" which the victims would take.

Next, we were taken to two symbolic cemeteries overflowing with tombstones of every size and description. Strangely, there did not seem to be any inscription on these stones. On a hillock between the two cemeteries, a

2. A pseudonym.

cold wind was forcing several trees to bend to its strength. The caretaker told us that bodies were buried beneath the trees and the force of nature would often cause human ashes and fragments to rise to the surface. We were then taken to a huge "burning pit." According to Kuryluk, there would be alternate layers of railroad ties and gassed bodies built up into a pyre which would then be set ablaze to dispose of the corpses.

The entire setting made my imagination run riot. I could not comprehend that some individual or some group had made the hideous decision that Jews, Poles, Gypsies or other "undesirables" had to be eradicated from the human race. I visualized hordes of people brought in an unending procession of trains for the express purpose of being annihilated: sealed cattle cars carrying the "dregs" from the East and luxury trains from the West bringing wealthy Jews from Holland, France and other countries. Since the victims arrived half-starved or already dead, it was an easy matter to run them through the "slough" (the death corridor) into the death chamber itself; those who were reluctant were "encouraged" with whips.

The words of a Russian military correspondent, Vasili Grossman, come to mind. He described the inferno, the catastrophe, of Treblinka in terms that defy the imagination. He spoke of flames issuing from the burning human bodies tens of meters high into the black sky and the sickening stench enveloping some ten kilometers, the terrible smell chasing the peasants from their homes. We were getting chilled from the cold wind and the effect on our emotions, and I regretted that I had left my raincoat in the cab. While alongside the burning pit, Kuryluk had pointed to a human ash which looked like a rotten egg shell. He invited me to take it as a "souvenir." I was filled with revulsion at the thought of it and this had added to my own chill.

Before we left the killing grounds, we questioned Kuryluk about the man known as "Ivan the Terrible." The caretaker had interviewed a number of witnesses who had seen and known the *real* Ivan. He declared that according to the witnesses, the huge Ivan had a most unusual walk or gait, swaggering with his elbows pumping back and forth. He imitated this walk and likened it to that of a sailor strutting down the street, yet with rounded shoulders, similar to that of a gorilla. He also noted that the real Ivan had thick eyebrows that did not separate over the nose. The description seemed very significant and it was not to be the first time that we were to hear it.

We next went to the home of Eugenia Samuel, a hoped-for defense witness, who had been incarcerated in Treblinka at the same time that the real Ivan the Terrible was present. Mrs. Samuel lived in Dorf Wolka Okroglik, a village about one kilometer from Treblinka. As we reached the gate, Mr. Samuel, accompanied by a barking dog, came from the fields to greet us. Mrs. Samuel was not home, but her husband invited us into the small building. Congenial and talkative, Mr. Samuel had no objection to my placing a tape recorder on the dining room table. A tall, lanky man with pipe in mouth, he spoke in generalities, and I soon turned off the recorder. His best suggestion was that we visit his brother-in-law in Warsaw, Josef Wujek, who had also been a Treblinka prisoner and survivor.

We returned to Warsaw that night in a driving rain and went to Wujek's home. Mrs. Wujek answered the door and called to her husband. A short, balding man with a round head and pleasant expression and wearing faded, striped pajamas, he looked like the stereotype of a concentration camp inmate. They graciously admitted us and immediately brought forth food and drink. Although willing to talk, the Wujeks would not consent to being photographed nor would they sign a statement.

Speaking in a calm, dispassionate voice, Wujek stated that he had reason to know and remember the *real* Ivan the Terrible, the beatings he had received at Ivan's hands an important aid to his recollections of the brutal guard. While riding his bicycle in the outskirts of Treblinka one day, Wujek had the misfortune to collide with Ivan, who was leading a horse-driven wagon laden with supplies. An altercation ensued and, infuriated, the evil Ivan grabbed the small, callow Wujek and incarcerated him in the Treblinka compound. This incident occurred during the early days of the Treblinka operation and Wujek, who was not a Jew, had the opportunity to observe Ivan frequently. After his release, Wujek was again arrested for a minor transgression during the summer of 1943, just before the famed uprising, and once more had the opportunity to study his nemesis. Wujek's description of the real Ivan coincided with those that I was to hear repeatedly. Ivan was a giant of a man, well over John Demjanjuk's approximate six feet. He was darkskinned and had bushy hair, bulging eyes with heavy eyebrows that did not separate, a grimace for a facial expression, and a shuffling walk that seemed to compensate for his burly size. His fellow guards were terrified of him, and Ivan once smashed the camera of a comrade who tried to take his photograph.

Wujek did not know if Ivan was killed during the uprising, or if he was able to escape before the Russian assault forces arrived. Wujek's most powerful statement was his estimate of Ivan's age, thirty-seven to forty, which would have been almost double that of the twenty-two-year-old youth, John Demjanjuk. Wujek also asserted repeatedly that the real Ivan had a constant, distorted look of "agitation and aggravation" which could very well indicate a highly disturbed psychotic, not at all like the serene-looking Demjanjuk.

Mark O'Connor told me that he had made arrangements for both Josef Wujek and Eugenia Samuel to come to the United States and then to Israel in order to make their depositions regarding the misidentification of John Demjanjuk. A third witness named Swistak unfortunately had died. However, a State Department functionary took it upon himself to notify the Office of Special Investigations (OSI) of this plan. The visas for these two people, which had been approved, were suddenly and mysteriously cancelled with no explanation, lending credence to the charge that the OSI withholds and hides exculpatory evidence.

CHAPTER TWO - HISTORY

As a high school student, my knowledge of Ukraine was a net zero. My teacher ignored it, describing it as either an extremely fertile area or a region owned equally by Russia and Poland. Only years later was I to learn that Ukraine was not a mere geographical concept, but rather a nation in its own right. Once known as Kievan Rus, not to be confused with Russia, Ukraine is larger than France. It lies due south and west of Russia. Its western borders extend into the Carpathian Mountains where it touches Poland, Hungary and Czechoslovakia. In the south, it borders Romania and the Black Sea. It has a population of more than fifty million people and recently celebrated its millennium of Christianity. The lack of mountains, rivers, or other clearly defined borders to serve as a natural defense line have been the main cause of Ukraine's tragic history.

This beautiful land has had a bloody history, from early in-fighting among Slavic tribes to invasions by Tatars, Turks, Mongols, Poles, Germans and Russians. After a brief period of freedom in 1917-18, deadly Russian horsemen coursed in from the north and hauled down the splendid blue and gold, tridentate Ukrainian flag. Again, the country was prisoner to an outsider.

A few years of peace ensued, but the paranoid Russians looked upon the population of farmers and middle classes as a threat to their concept of collectivization. The existence of capitalism and personal ownership of land was, in Communist eyes, a grave problem to be dealt with, one that required drastic measures. The Russian solution was to cause an intentional famine as a measure of national policy. Thus, in 1932-33, this richest of agricultural lands, the bread-basket of Europe, was starved to death. Many of its anguished people resorted even to cannibalism in their torment.

In this hideous atmosphere, John Demjanjuk was about twelve years old. Somehow, he managed to survive. Although he lost most of his family, he was sturdy and managed to sustain himself on wild berries and scraps until some semblance of normality returned. Anyone who could survive such an experience could well survive any future terror no matter how bizarre.

Meanwhile, diabolic machinations were occurring in the international arena that would thrust civilization into World War II. The Russians and Germans colluded on the infamous Molotov-Von Ribbentrop Treaty to give each other time to arm and to decide how they would carve up Europe to their mutual satisfaction. What most people are not aware of is that the Russians were fortifying heavily along their western border, and some experts believe that this is what led the Nazis to strike first. Germany invaded Poland in 1939, and England and France then declared war on the Nazi military machine.

Young John was drafted into the Red Army in 1942, Russian Soviets having found use for Ukrainian peasants even if only as cannon fodder. The boy initially was rejected by the army because he did not have a change of underwear, but after atoning for this shortcoming, he was finally accepted. Suffering a wound in combat, he was hospitalized for a short time, then sent back to the front until he was eventually taken prisoner by the Germans during the Battle of Kerch in the spring of 1942.

At the southernmost part of the Soviet Union that juts into the Black Sea lies the huge Crimean peninsula, a land mass with a small peninsula of its own called the Kerch peninsula which extends east towards the mainland. Looking somewhat like New York's Long Island, it is roughly one hundred kilometers long and, at its most narrow point, twelve kilometers wide. This was the setting entitled "Operation Bustard" by the Nazis for the extraordinary Battle of Kerch.

Some 25,000 German troops faced a force of 200,000 Soviet soldiers. Under ordinary circumstances, such an array would suggest a German slaughter. After sporadic shooting and killing, the Germans made a strategic retreat of some eighty miles when, to their amazement, the Soviets began to drop their weapons, surrendering en masse to the Nazis. After a campaign of only ten days, this astonishing spectacle of thousands of the voluntarily defeated holding hands and marching unresistingly towards their Teutonic conquerors was to be repeated many times over until, in the end, five million Soviets had been taken prisoner. The symbolism of such surrender would seem to be proof positive of the loathing felt by the Russians and Ukrainians against their Communist slave-masters. Certainly, the Nazis might have put to better use this overwhelming Soviet manpower. On the other hand, capture and imprisonment by the Germans might not be as bad as being under the thumb of the hated Soviet Russians.

John Demjanjuk was first imprisoned at Rovno in Ukraine, then taken to the giant POW camp at Chelm, in eastern Poland near the Soviet border. Thousands were "processed" at this camp, some forcibly and some eagerly, in order to join the German assault against the Communist oppressor. Surprisingly, the Nazis then arrogantly used starvation as a convenient way to thin out the prison population and some 200,000 Russian and Ukrainian POWs perished.

By a stroke of luck, John reached Chelm at the same time that the Nazis had decided to end their starvation policy and had begun to give the POWs enough rations to sustain life. Since John was tall and husky, and able to withstand the rigors of the POW camp, the Germans used him for forced labor. Digging peat and working on an agricultural estate at Okszow, he was then put on a railroad section gang, assigned to repair railroad tracks.

During my interviews with John at the Ayalon prison in Israel, he was very emphatic about this railroad work, also mentioning that eventually he was given an Italian uniform and a gun, though he never had occasion to use it. It is such personally-related detail that he remembers clearly, rather than specific dates or the names of fellow inmates or officials supervising the camp that the prosecution has made such an issue of. What, after all, is such a camp other than a large tract of land with a fence around it and patrolling guards, with enormous numbers of emaciated, starving men keeling over every day? Why would one bother to remember the name of one man when there would be others like him standing next to you the next day? Within the framework of such an atmosphere, such impersonal detail becomes meaningless. What he does recall is that he spent approximately eighteen months at Chelm. Taken prisoner in the spring of 1942, and continuously incarcerated until his release from Chelm in the spring of 1944, there is no way that he could have been at Treblinka, which was only in operation between the summer of 1942 and the summer of 1943.

Impressed by his work as a forced laborer, and in light of the fact that he wanted to fight Stalin's Communist forces, the German authorities eventually sent Demjanjuk to join the Vlasovites Army at Graz. It is imperative to understand that the Nazis absolutely would not permit an ex-POW who had served as a concentration camp guard under the S.S. to join the Vlasovites Army since they had a very real fear that ex-KZ guards might be taken prisoner and talk about the mass exterminations they had witnessed. Their paybooks even carried a special endorsement to that effect. Demjanjuk's attorney in the extradition proceedings, Mark O'Connor, immediately saw the significance of this fact, recognizing that it could destroy the false evidence against Demjanjuk. Unfortunately, his present attorney, Yoram Sheftel, in closing arguments did a grave disservice to his client by stating that, "his stay in the Vlasov Army is not the heart of his alibi."[3]

After Graz, John was posted to Camp Heuberg, some forty miles south of Stuttgart, which was a secondary training center. He was familiar with nearby Munsingen and Bad Reichenhall, two other Vlasovites recruitment and

---

3. *The Jerusalem Post,* February 27, 1988. All excerpts are taken from the international edition except where otherwise noted.

training centers, and for a short time, he was bodyguard for Vlasovite General Feodor Trukhin. I was struck by the casual way in which John mentioned his service as bodyguard to the officer directly under General Vlasov, not realizing the enormous significance of it.

After the war, Demjanjuk was admitted to a series of DP camps. A photograph shows him as a sentry in one of them, indicating a very slender, ordinary-looking man who appears to be anything but the burly, bruising Ivan of Treblinka. The DP records indicate a stay at Danzig, up north on the Baltic Sea in the area previously known as the Polish Corridor. In a listing of DP camps where he resided, we note Landshut where he had an operation and Regensburg where he was married to his wife, Vera. Finally, he was at Feldafing, a bizarre U.S. POW camp presided over by German prisoners.

In West Germany, John was trained by the U.S. Army of Occupation, then hired to work as a truck driver. Because of his contribution to our forces and his unblemished record, he was accepted into the U.S. DP program and eventually emigrated to the United States in 1952.

The Demjanjuks settled in Cleveland, Ohio, and John secured employment with the Ford Motor Company which, even after his many years of service to it, never lifted a finger to help its devoted employee when he desperately needed it. Neither did the U.A.W. In Cleveland, the Demjanjuks were quickly integrated into the suburban Seven Hills community. They were active in church work and community affairs, and John enjoyed a hobby of making wine which he gave away to his friends, as he never drank alcohol himself.

Thirty-five years of this happy life in Cleveland made John proud that he and his family were American citizens. This man, accused of being an archcriminal, was guilty of only one offense during all those years, a ticket for a traffic violation.

During this peaceful period while John and Vera were rearing their three children, something ominous was brewing. It was as though fate were manipulating events to ensnare John deliberately as the central figure in a horrific drama that would occupy center stage before a world audience. At the time they occurred, these events would seem to have had no bearing on this man with a fourth-grade education who had, in the words of Yoram Sheftel, " the intelligence of a child of ten."[4]

It is impossible to give an encapsulated picture of a man s life, no way to describe the maddening and excruciating hunger pains of his youth while he watched friends and relatives die in the inglorious Ukraine famine; while he suffered the wounds of battle and endured the torment of sleeping on frozen

4. The Jerusalem Post daily edition, February 27, 1988

ground as a POW at Chelm and saw his fellow prisoners starve and freeze to death; and while living a constant cycle of imprisonment, all culminating in a trial more appropriate to the Middle Ages.

CHAPTER THREE-THE PLOT THICKENS

As the lines for the foundation of an incredible conspiracy were being drawn, a most improbable but deadly role was being played by former New York Congresswoman Elizabeth Holtzman, herself of Jewish-Ukrainian extraction. While a member of Congress and during the closing session, she secured passage of a law that in effect established a "Nazi-hunting unit" that ostensibly would bring to heel all the Nazis residing in the United States, and secondarily end various forms of discrimination. Congress passed her law and added the appendage known as the Office of Special Investigations (OSI) to the United States Department of Justice.

This agency is funded with well over $3 million per year, its sole function being to chase down Nazis and deport or extradite them, primarily to the USSR or Israel. Since we have no law that deals per se with war criminal trials, the OSI is reduced to searching for flaws in visa applications as its only excuse to deport people. But, one might ask, who would not submit a doctored resume to avoid being shipped back to a country where the end result is execution? Who would want to risk the lives of relatives still residing in the old country to death or imprisonment? Why are we selective and go after the hundreds of thousands of ex-refugees who have falsified their visas for these reasons? What do we do about the hundreds of thousands of refugees who have entered this country without visas?

The OSI has earned its sordid reputation because it is the only American agency that works hand-in-hand with the KGB, the Russian Secret Police. It wholeheartedly accepts "evidence" about so-called war criminals from the Soviet Union, the most untrustworthy source in the world, a country that has made a specialty of lies, deception and forgery. With little or no conscience, the OSI has a proclivity towards targeting the innocent as well as the guilty, the classic example being an unsuccessful attempt to criminalize Frank Walus, a Polish-American who had himself been a prisoner of the Nazis. In a vicious, drummed-up accusation, Walus was fingered as the "Butcher of Kielce," a Gestapo murderer who slew countless victims. Twelve "witnesses" were rehearsed, flown from Israel to the United States and testified – under oath – that Walus was guilty of the butchery. Strangely, it was alleged that all of these witnesses save one had migrated directly from Russia to Israel without even having seen Poland. How could they have accurately testified about Kielce?

We must ask ourselves that if twelve persons were so mistaken or had deliberately lied in the Walus case, why is it not possible that the five prosecution witnesses in the Demjanjuk case were equally not believable, especially since they were directed by the same Israeli/OSI controllers? A most disgusting aspect of this unwarranted tactic was the fact that Walus himself was a wartime prisoner of the Germans. We wonder why these witnesses were not jailed for perjury and the grief they caused Walus?

It is now understandable why the Israeli court was so adamant in its refusal to make a connection between the two cases. It was eventually discovered that Walus was a Pole, not a German; therefore, he could not have been accepted as a member of the Gestapo. The OSI reaction to the smearing of this man who even had acid thrown in his face on the Chicago Courthouse steps was merely to say, "We made a mistake." A bureaucracy not averse to peering into coffins in its eager search for people and bodies that might be ex-Nazis, the OSI focused on setting up a major symbol of the Jewish Holocaust. Guilt or innocence being irrelevant, the important question is why John Demjanjuk was selected to be this symbol, especially since his name had never been on any Nazi-criminal list.

This fateful event began innocently enough. John's wife Vera decided to take a trip to the old country. Neither saw any reason for concern, much less danger. She had not served in the Red Army; she had not surrendered to the Germans; she had not violated the "bullet order" which prescribes that a Russian soldier must always save one last bullet to kill himself rather than be taken prisoner. And she did not serve in the Vlasov Army. There was no risk; she was only a housewife.

. According to Attorney O'Connor, who frequently visited the Demjanjuk family in Cleveland, Vera's first visit to Ukraine was to John's mother who was shocked to discover that her son was still alive, as she had been collecting a mother's veteran pension for all these years. After Vera left, the delighted old lady went to the KGB and joyously told them, "You don't have to pay me a pension anymore; my boy is alive and living in Cleveland, Ohio." On hearing this incredible admission, the KGB immediately invaded her house and confiscated all photographs and documents pertaining to John. The machinery of a police state began to operate.

Shortly thereafter, in September 1977, *News From Ukraine,* a notorious English-language Communist newspaper located in New York City, published a lengthy article describing John Demjanjuk as a "traitor to the Motherland" because he had violated the bullet-order. This was all the OSI needed: it had its symbol. The OSI quickly swung into action, transmogrifying the "traitor to the Motherland" into the man who singlehandedly slaughtered innumerable Jews, ranging from 850,000 to 1,200,000 at Treblinka. In short order, the OSI felt, Demjanjuk would be denaturalized, i.e., stripped of his U.S. citizenship, and deported to the Soviet Union for swift execution. However, since extradition takes precedence over deportation, the OSI had another trial in store for it where the receiving country would be Israel instead of the Soviet Union.

Demjanjuk's denaturalization trial in Cleveland was presided over by Frank Battisti, Chief Judge of the US District Court, a man who himself had been under investigation by a Federal Grand Jury for two years. Even though that legal proceeding ended in a hung jury, ten judges had stood up against Battisti in an effort to restrict him to administrative duties. Because John's trial was a civil action rather than a criminal one, he was not entitled to free legal services; thus, money became a serious problem. His first lawyer was inept, and he was discharged. Nor was there a jury and, along with the domination of a questionable judge, the situation was very appealing to the OSI Eventually, Mark O'Connor was brought into the case. The Demjanjuk family had been enormously impressed with the late Dr. O'Connor and felt that his son would provide an aggressive defense and gain ultimate freedom for John.

John was denaturalized because of the inaccurate information on his U.S. visa application. There was no mention of Nazi allegations nor was anything said about the thousands of other former refugees who had "lied" on their visas because they were terrified of being shipped back to the Soviet Union, or because of their very real fear of retribution against relatives still living there.

Although the partially inaccurate residential data on the visa was the crux of the case against John, the prosecution cleverly developed the cloud of Nazism in its presentation so as to influence and muddy their charge against him. This was a reprehensible tactic exceeded only by the Israeli court's unwarranted recapitulation of World War II horrors to provide an incriminating and unethical framework for Demjanjuk's eventual conviction. John Demjanjuk the individual was on trial, one must understand, not World War II or the spectre of Nazism.

Some of the Nazi "business," although not the essence of the charge, dealt with the strange identity card which the Israeli authorities would later and ill-advisedly attempt to use as the linchpin of their case against John. Battisti admitted to O'Connor that he knew the matter of the forged card was critically important in the trial, yet went ahead with the denaturalization and deportation procedures under OSI and KGB pressure. When O'Connor called for justice,

Battisti threatened to jail him.

Mark O'Connor had been called into the case late in the game and could not know the odds against him. He could not anticipate such actions as our U.S. Marshals surrounding the floodlit Cleveland home of Demjanjuk, or the needless handcuffing of the astonished victim, or even their striking John's daughter, Lydia. The appalled attorney rushed to Cleveland and immediately had John released. One is forced to conclude that such actions of the U.S. Marshals were more like those of Nazi Germany or Stalinist Russia. But most unfortunate of all, O'Connor could not undo the damage wrought by the first lawyer who lost the denaturalization portion of the proceedings. John Demjanjuk was no longer an American citizen and could not be more vulnerable.

As we reflect on the building of the conspiracy, we are constantly reminded that Demjanjuk had ample opportunities to skip across the border to Canada if he were guilty of anything. But what need did he have to run, to abandon his family?

Trying to put into perspective the job that was done on John in the city of Cleveland under the aegis of a strange judge who himself had made questionable headlines, we recall another unusual event. In this allegation, the first defense attorney for Demjanjuk and an associate traveled to Hamburg, Germany, to meet with former Trawniki Commandant, Karl Streibel, in order to arrange for three witnesses to come to the U.S. to clear John. The pair arrived on a Monday and an appointment was made for the following Tuesday afternoon. In the interim, the U.S. attorney received a mysterious phone call wherein he was told that Streibel did not want to see him. At the same time, Streibel received a call telling him that the American was canceling the interview.[5] The lawyer and his associate returned to the U.S. empty-handed. Some days later, he phoned Streibel at 2 a.m. "Why did you not meet with me?" Streibel asked. Comparing notes, the two suddenly realized that a deception had been played upon them. It was alleged that the OSI's Michael Wolff then stopped the visas of the three witnesses who could clear John. The OSI was doing a beautiful job. It commanded a show trial of the highest order in Cleveland, Ohio. It fingered, then proceeded to attack John Demjanjuk as the flashiest symbol of the Holocaust since Eichmann. Its next step would be to close the triad with Israel as the third leg.

5. My source for this information wishes to remain anonymous.

CHAPTER FOUR - IN JAIL

After the denaturalization, deportation and extradition procedures, John was taken to a Federal prison in Springfield, Missouri, where he was confined for a year and a half in a tiny cell with little light and no fresh air. When he emerged, he was gaunt and pale, a shadow of his former self. Rushed to New York City's Kennedy airport without even being permitted to see his family, he was packed off to Israel, his one "break," rather than to Russia where a "traitor to the Motherland" would have been shot on arrival.

When he landed in Israel, John was immediately put into solitary confinement at Ayalon prison in the dusty old town of Ramle, about a half hour's drive from Jerusalem. It is a semi-rural area with old houses and rusty farm machinery abandoned by the wayside, the only relief provided by an abundance of trees and shrubbery. As the prison comes into view, the flowing colors of red, orange, and yellow paint on the walls make you think of an amusement park.

Warden Peretz Chen is a Sephardic Jew from North Africa. During our first visit to the prison, Mark O'Connor and I were seated at a long table and a prisoner brought us refreshments. The prisoner was evidently well-liked and regarded with amusement by the warden and his associates. The warden explained that this man got into some mischief in Hungary, but escaped. Fearful of being deported, he stole a car so he would be imprisoned in Israel. However, he was trusted and made an orderly. After this bit of hospitality, which would be repeated on subsequent visits, we were escorted to John's cell.

Our first impression of the isolation cell was that of a large room. To the right, three guards were posted with Uzis. One of them sat at a desk at the far right, staring at floor-to-ceiling bars on our left. Directly behind him was a TV camera mounted on the wall, also aimed at the bars, and a spotlight was focused on the cell. A guard posted at the door moved a small table to the edge of the bars so that we could sit in comfort while speaking with Demjanjuk. Looking to the left, we saw John, clutching at the bars, joyful at seeing us. Talking nonstop, he vividly described the conditions, the harassment by interrogators, and his appraisal of his situation. The police investigators, usually three at a time, would come three or four days a week and alternately cajole or threaten him to "plead guilty." "Why should I plead guilty?" he would demand. "I have done nothing that I am guilty of!"

John was confined for nearly a year without being charged with a crime, which we understand is against Israeli law, and many decent Israelis have been upset by this illegality. When the trial eventually began, John was transported daily from Ayalon to the Jerusalem courthouse in manacles and shackles, traveling eighty kilometers in a speeding van up and down hills and around curves at breakneck speed. With no support he was often slammed to the floor, sustaining injuries to his body and arriving at court in tears from the excruciating pain.

John Demjanjuk is burly, about six feet tall, but has a mild demeanor, and speaks lovingly of his wife and children, his church and his community in Ohio. He is gratified by the thousands of cards and letters that have poured in to him.

When his family were allowed to visit him the first time, John delightedly held his infant grandson, Eddie, and burst out singing in a booming basso voice that made the air vibrate with its power and beauty.

During my several interviews with John, I was impressed by the fact that he kept returning to the matter of his service in the Vlasov Army. Since I did not initiate this subject, it would seem to substantiate the truth and veracity of his claim that he had been a member of the army. I was aware that as early as 1942, certain Soviet military men were collaborating on the idea of siding with the Germans, not to advance Nazism but to free their enslaved homeland. As military strategists, they saw the necessity for a staging area, strong logistical support and a strong ally. There was no alternative other than to turn to Nazi Germany.

In a personal letter to the author from Count Nikolai Tolstoy, the brilliant English historian, he calls attention to material held by Vlasovite Colonel Konstantin Kromiadi "which goes far to bear out Demjanjuk's story." According to Tolstoy, this material was given to Attorney Sheftel, who has not used it. According to expert military historians, it is important to understand that General Andre Vlasov and his troops were anything but Nazis. Although allied with the German military machine, the Vlasovites manifested themselves philosophically as strong Russian nationalists and refused to participate in any anti-Semitic activity.

Sadly, Israel is the focal point for the John Demjanjuk case. Many authorities insist that Israel was reluctant to become involved in this matter and acquiesced only under pressure by the American government as personified by the OSI. It is indeed suspect that the OSI has the need to maintain a branch office in Tel Aviv to help supervise the proceedings seemingly from arrest to execution. But as long as they were stuck with this hot potato, Israel proceeded to make the best of it. In terms of motivation, vengeance and revenge against a hated symbol of the Holocaust are a given in Israel.

Additionally, this was a great opportunity to operate an "educational" program so that Israel's young would never forget the Holocaust and its ramifications. Israeli authorities have admitted that this was a prime reason for holding the Demjanjuk trial, and a practice was made of busing thousands of school children and young soldiers to witness it.

Jacob Youngman, a retired Jewish businessman and Treblinka survivor, has declared:

> *I feel that although many Jews were killed, the numbers these leaders use are false. Whenever anyone makes money off figures, they tend to increase them. Don't forget that the truly unique thing about the murder of Jews in the second world war is not the numbers that were killed but the institution that has been built up around this tragedy. Numbers do not mean a lot. Many people play with numbers. I saw many people die in the camps: Jews, Catholics, German criminals, soldiers accused of cowardice. I saw many people die, but they were people, not just Jews* [6]

In effect, then, the elements of a "show trial" were falling into place. The United States had done its "duty" even though it involved persecuting an innocent man, violating its own constitution and interfering in the affairs of a foreign power. Israel was happy to present the "Satanic Majesty of the Holocaust," starring John Demjanjuk as chief operator of one of its most notorious death camps and on the stage of a music hall theater which substituted for a courtroom where some three hundred people, many of whom waited in line for hours to gain admittance, swarmed amid police, soldiers, press and TV cameras.

The shadow of a pleased Russia was always present: it prepared an artistic forged I.D. card for Israel that would supposedly doom Demjanjuk, and it used an agreeable messenger, one Armand Hammer, to deliver it to Jerusalem. Many people are in agreement that in return for Russia's release of thousands of Jewish refuseniks to Israel for demographic purposes, Israel would act as hatchetman to destroy Demjanjuk.

Israeli citizens repeatedly told me of the justice and impartiality of their judges, that they were fair and had the ability to disregard any potential prejudice or discrimination by the media or the courtroom audiences. But the

6. Jacob Youngman, *The Spotlight* (Washington, D.C., April 28, 1986) pg. 6

three judges of the Demjanjuk trial — Chief Judge Dov Levin, known as a "hanging judge"; Zvi Tal, the religious judge; and Dalia Dorner, woman judge — found him guilty even before his plane touched down on Israeli territory.

CHAPTER FIVE - THE I.D. CARD

In order to reach the wrongful conviction of Ukrainian-American John Demjanjuk of Cleveland, Ohio, as Ivan the Terrible of Treblinka, the government of Israel hung its hat on three points: the notorious I.D. card supposedly issued at the Nazi training camp in Trawniki, Poland; the forty-five-year-old memories of aged "witnesses" who allegedly were inmates and survivors of Treblinka ; and the matter of John's whereabouts during the period for which he was being tried.

The full significance of the I.D. card was made forcefully clear by Barbara Amouyal, a *Jerusalem Post* reporter, in a hard-hitting interview of attorney Mark O'Connor. O'Connor declared that both Valeri Kubanov, the first secretary of the Soviet Embassy, and Judge Frank Battisti admitted that "key evidence against him [Demjanjuk] had been 'doctored' and further admitted that they knew of the forgeries, yet proceeded with Demjanjuk's deportation hearings in light of OSI and KGB pressure."[7] Quoting further from Amouyal's interview:

O'Connor also claimed that experts had determined that the Nazis normally photographed people at an angle, and not full-face, so that the ear and profile could be used as identifying features. The picture on Demjanjuk's I.D. card was full-face. Further, O'Connor said, experts had said the photograph had been air-brushed to erase an identification tag over the left pocket, as well as buttons at the throat and pocket flap. The writing on the card is not even German; it's...Slavic. Also, if you look closely, you'll see this is a standard Red Army tunic, and not a German Nazi Uniform.

O'Connor related to me that he had met with Kubanov at the Soviet Embassy in Washington and Kubanov had admitted to him, in effect: "Of course we altered the I.D. card. This is an internal Soviet matter. It is nobody else's business." O'Connor told us that he immediately reported this conversation to the office of William Webster, head of the F.B.I. at the time, but never received a response.

7. The *Jerusalem Post*, March 24, 1986.

When O'Connor and I met with Rudolf Reiss, who served as paymaster at the Trawniki training camp from December 1941 to August 1943 and who now lives in Hamburg, Reiss expressed amazement on seeing a copy of the I.D. card used in the trial. Having processed some 5,000 such cards at Trawniki, Reiss declared he had never seen one like the card in the Demjanjuk case, and he denounced this particular card as an absurdity.[8]

Antonio Canto, a U.S. government document expert trained in both physics and chemistry and with a history of having examined more than 10,000 kinds of paper and ink in his investigations, testified that he found "six different kinds of ink for writing and one type of ink for all the stamps imprinted on the I.D. card." There was no recognition of the possibility that in the midst of a savage war, it is difficult to visualize a small, German clerical staff rushing to and fro to procure six kinds of ink for one I.D. card.

Forensic expert Edna Robertson demonstrated that when the two halves of the I.D. were folded together, the left side was larger than the right; she noted also that the stamps appeared to be composed of two different halves; and she emphasized that the stamps were of different colors in each of the two parts.

Judge Levin reacted only to the changes in color by quoting from the words of Captain Amnon Bezaleli, head of the laboratory for documents investigation at Israeli police headquarters: "It seems that with the passage of years the color of the stamp on the photograph changed, due to the effect of the photography material." Continuing with his source, Bezaleli, Levin stated that "the characteristics in both parts of the stamps [plural] are identical...,and then he concluded that "the photograph slipped off after it had been stamped and was glued on again, and that the discrepancy was created because of inaccuracy in gluing." The judge also saw fit to say that although Bezaleli could not determine that the I.D. card and other Trawniki documents were typed with the same typewriter, "he found that the typing in these four above mentioned documents was with a typewriter of the same make - Olympia model 1930."[9]

---

8. In the course of completing this book, we learned that Mr. Reiss and his wife paid a visit to the U.S. in November 1988. In the past, he had been welcomed with open arms so that he could participate in the Cleveland Trials of John Demjanjuk and make a historical contribution. Since then, he has been put on the government's watch list. When he arrived at Kennedy Airport in New York, he was immediately arrested, handcuffed and jailed overnight while his wife went into hysterics. The next day, they were bundled on a plane and sent back to Germany.

9. State of Israel vs. Ivan (John) Demjanjuk Verdict, pg 0640 Criminal Case No 373/B6. *In The Jerusalem Court*. With a special bench in terms of the Courts Act (offenses carrying the death penalty) 5721 - 1961.

We do not understand the relevance of the last statement. We also do not know if the Olympia was a post-war machine, a fact which would mitigate toward John's innocence. Although the paper used for the I.D. card was readily available in the year 1941, no recognition was given to the possibility that that would not stop the Russians from confiscating tons of paper after the war just as they confiscated everything else of value, including machinery, entire factories and trainloads of oil, etc.

Julius Grant, internationally recognized forensic expert from England, called attention to two rust marks on the identity card which were caused by staples. Since there had never been a stapler at Trawniki, he concluded that "the document got into the hands of the Russians and it was therefore not signed at Trawniki, but in Russia." In other words, Streibel's signature was forged.

William Flynn, Chief Documents Examiner for the State of Arizona and one of ten people who sit on a national board that certifies documents examiners, demonstrated the ease of forgery by forging the signatures of two German officers himself. After comparing the letters "D" and "YA" in Demjanjuk's signature to those of the Trawniki card, it was his conclusion that if the Demjanjuk signature was a forgery, then the entire card was a forgery.

Flynn also tried in vain to present a photo montage to show how easily a photo forgery can be made in order to demonstrate that the photo on the Trawniki card was composed of one person's head and the torso of another. But the judges refused to accept this as evidence as they also refused the results of an iron ion-migration test that established how long the ink had been on the Trawniki card. Their excuse was that Flynn had not included details of the test in his written report. It is interesting that at a later date, August 22, 1988, Flynn wrote a searing denunciation of OSI Director Neal Sher for making false allegations about Flynn's testimony.

Dieter Lehner of Bavaria, a professional documents examiner and graphic artist, has written a book about the asinine "documentation" that was used against John Demjanjuk, and travels the world in an effort to secure justice for him. It is noteworthy that Lehner's duties are to analyze official stamps, seals, signatures, titles and dates in a wide variety of governmental documents, some dating back to the Prussian era. Significantly, part of his job is to distinguish genuine Nazi memorabilia from the vast amount of commercial and political

---

Before the Honorable Judges: Dov Levin, Judge of the Supreme Court, Zvi A. Tal, Dalia Dorner.

All quotations taken from the Verdict are from the English version.

forgeries that have emerged throughout the world since the end of the war. In his book, *Thou Shalt Not Bear False Witness*, Lehner states that,

> *unlike standard Nazi documents of the time, the card was not made on a linotype machine [but] is a hand-made document, the lines beneath the data were made with a damaged ruler and each straight line on the card had tiny V-shaped flaws, all identical. . . .*

Also that,

> *the colons and umlauts were not identical which means that they were hand-set, and that the card contains two seals from diverse agencies in the Third Reich – agencies so different in purpose that their seals never appeared together on any authentic document.*

And further, that

> *the seal on the upper part of the card . . . is that of a police official. The one on the lower half . . . belonged to an S.S. political officer.*[10]

There are other anomalies that have been pointed out by experts such as the fact that there is neither a date of issue nor a date of expiration on the card. Furthermore, it does not have Demjanjuk's signature under the photograph, nor does it have the signature of the issuing official under the place where Demjanjuk's signature should have been. It has no title page in front, and the data are rubber stamped whereas authentic I.D. cards have the data printed on them. The rubber stamp heading, indicating the camp location, has been found on no other I.D. card, and if such a card were intended for widespread use, other cards with this heading would have surfaced by now. If the card were intended only to be used within Trawniki, the heading would have been printed in rather than being stamped on.

John's eyes are indicated as being gray rather than their actual blue, his light blond hair is described as dark blond, and his height is off by 12 cm.

There is no distinct number on the rectangular white patch over the left chest of the man in the photo and the white disc below the patch is of the wrong size and shape. Shadows on the face suggest overhead lighting but the shadows

---

10. Dieter Lehner, *Du Sollst nicht falsch Zeugnis geben* (*Thou Shalt Not Bear False Witness*) , Berg Am See : Kurt Vowinckel-Verlag,1987.

on neck and collar indicate that the light comes from a horizontal direction, suggesting that the upper and lower parts of the photograph belong to different individuals.

Both photo and stamps show signs of removal and reattachment, which leads one to suspect that a different photo and different stamps were substituted. The photo has two vertical staple marks indicating that it had been previously attached to another document, and since military photos were either glued on or fastened with grommets, one can only wonder at the use of staples. There is glue on the back of the photo but there is evidence of two distinct glues.

The printing job is slovenly, a questionable disparity in view of the obsessive neatness of the Germans. There is no printer's code, and there is an incomprehensible mixture of linotype and handset sections on the same page, multiple and varied fonts rather than one standard print, and the use of a rare non-German font. The font style is Latin instead of Gothic, and the German shortcut of writing a double "ess" by using a letter that looks like an English capital "B" with a little "tail" and slightly slanted to the right is not used at all.

The gross misuse of terminology on the card would appall anyone familiar with the German language, and is found only on Demjanjuk's card and on no other Nazi-German document or identification. Furthermore, there are word usages that did not even exist during World War II such as *Essgeschirr,* now meaning "eating utensil," and which evolved in the late 1960s and was not even incorporated into German and Russian dictionaries until the early 1970s. How such a word came to appear on the card during World War II when the commonly used expression for "cooking utensil" was *Essbestuck* is strange. There are also certain oddities, words that appear only on the Demjanjuk card and which often include unacceptable spelling errors that would make a German schoolboy laugh. And even umlauts, as much a part of the German language as any letter of the German alphabet, are left out or misused.

Experts also found the use of wrong or inappropriate seals. The seal on page one, for example, is totally different from the two seals on the corners of the picture on page two, which do not belong on that type of document in any case. Instead of a single, dotted circle, the seal guide ring on page one is shown as a double ring with a solid outer circle and a faint, irregular inner circle. Furthermore, the lightning bolt SS symbols on the seals are too slanted and appear to be drawn in. Most Nazi seals had a small number underneath the swastika wreath, but the seals on Demjanjuk's card lack those numbers.

The card, moreover, is in excellent condition for its age and for one supposedly carried around and used on a daily basis. Of critical importance, the card does not indicate that Demjanjuk was ever even sent to Treblinka, the issue for which he was tried. Odd, too, is that a German identity card would show one of their workers with a Soviet-style haircut and wearing a Soviet military work jacket. Furthermore, the card is made of paper whereas an authentic one was usually printed on oilcloth. German military issue is not typed on such cards, but this one is, the card stating furthermore that two coats were issued to Demjanjuk even though two coats would never have been issued to one individual.

No one denies that the face on the photo of the card resembles that of John. However, O'Connor found an official Soviet Ukrainian-language newspaper, *Molod Ukrainy,* published in early 1986, that shows a photo-identity card allegedly linking Demjanjuk to the Nazi death camps. This version of the card is identical to the one the Soviets gave to American and Israeli prosecutors, with one exception: it bears another man's photograph superimposed on the reverse side of the card in an area that was previously blank. This fact alone would seem to destroy any possible use of the I.D. card as "evidence."

It is a well known fact that Soviet authorities will leave original documents with American courts for only a short time. Not only does this make Soviet "evidence" highly suspect, it puts the American judiciary in the absurd position of having to use photocopies so that ink and typewriter ribbon cannot be tested. The original was flown from Moscow to Israel for "testing" by the good offices of the oil magnate, Armand Hammer,[11] but it is not unlikely that Moscow had plenty of time and opportunity to re-do the card.

The matter of the I.D. card is so obviously a mockery, so unquestionably a crude forgery that does nothing to establish an identification, that all it does is to prove beyond a shadow of a doubt that the trial was rigged and had a predetermined outcome. Someone once said that if you tell a big enough lie loud enough and long enough, people will accept it as the truth. This lie is so flagrant and so bizarre that it can only indicate desperation for a conviction.

It is nothing short of astounding that Michael Shaked, the prosecutor in Demjanjuk's trial - - a thin, angular, humorless man who would smile wryly

---

11. The *Jerusalem Post* daily edition, April 23, 1987 quoted Judge Levin as saying: If you want a different example, let's say the wind blew it in here. And what if that wind is called Armand Hammer, why is that not acceptable?"

whenever Chief Judge Dov Levin did his work for him by harassing and deprecating the defense lawyers and witnesses - - could even attempt to defend the validity of the I.D. card in the face of the professional competence of forensic experts accurately testifying for the defense.

One wonders if, in the carnage and terror of World War II, the Nazis would have even bothered to devise an elaborate sham of an I.D. card for one unimportant, ill-educated country boy of Ukrainian origin. Furthermore, it is inconceivable that a huge training camp like Trawniki would not have its own printshop to handle the 5,000 men processed through it and, instead, rely on a neighboring town to have adequate printing facilities.

When Levin admitted that Treblinka was not listed on the card as one of John's postings, why were the charges not immediately dismissed? Acknowledging the futility of using the discredited I.D. card, the ever inventive and intractable judge resigned himself to saying: ". . . the fate of the defendant [is] decided. . . on the basis of the survivors of Treblinka, in whose heart and head his image was imprinted."[12] He limps off with the weak and shallow comment that the I.D card is only "supporting" evidence. But really, what can it actually support, and what else can it do other than raise grave suspicions about the use of unsavory "evidence" to convict John Demjanjuk?

Although many years have gone by until the defendant reached his present age of 69, there is sardonic humor in Levin's observation that "John is one of those people whose face has not been affected by the aging process." But in spite of the effusive commentary on morphological and anatomical signs, photomontages, identification scales, and forensics, he still refused to recognize that an accurate photo was first attached, then re-attached to a blank I.D. card, and that the written changes were added at a later date. Nor does he consider the story about the "other" I.D. card, identical to John's forged one, that presented an entirely different face. Too many ridiculous games were played with this so-called "evidence" to make it of any value.

A supreme bit of irony is that while the Israeli Government is frantically attempting to finger Demjanjuk as the chief guard at Treblinka, the Russian authors of the absurd identity card say not a word about it. They are interested in Demjanjuk only as a "traitor to the Motherland" because he violated the infamous "bullet order," another of Stalin's stupid rules revealing his contempt for humanity in general and his own people in particular.

---

12. Verdict, pg. 0669

CHAPTER SIX - WITNESSES FOR THE PROSECUTION

Aware that the "evidence" of the so-called identity card had become a huge joke and a parody of justice, Chief Judge Dov Levin was forced to declare that "the verdict in this trial is based first and foremost on the testimony and statements of the identifying witnesses."[13] We must ask if they were truthful and honorable witnesses. All evidence in this trial establishes beyond a shadow of a doubt that they were not. They could not agree on something so simple and basic as the location of buildings and activities at Treblinka nor even on a map of Treblinka itself, which was composed of a labor camp as well as an extermination camp. One witness, Eliyahu Rosenberg, even refused to discuss the layout of the camp. There were even discrepancies in terms of guards' voices, location of facilities, and visibility of the two camps. We have to credit Attorney O'Connor for uncovering the lies, the collusions, the contradictions, and the fatal discrepancies in the witnesses' testimonies, and we have to credit Levin as the strategist and artisan who used elaborate and unacceptable snares and emotionalism to make a primitive ploughboy the Ukrainian symbol for the World War II Holocaust of the Jews, second only to the German Eichmann.

On August 2, 1943, the inmates of Treblinka rose up against their warders and attempted a mass breakout. In the words of expert source Jean-Francois Steiner, who made an intense, thorough and systematic research of the history of Death Camp Treblinka:

Of these six hundred escapees there remained, on the arrival of the Red Army a year later, only forty survivors. The others had been killed in the course of that year by Polish peasants, partisans of the Armia Krajowa, Ukrainian fascist bands, deserters from the Wehrmacht, the Gestapo, and special units of the German army. [14]

13. Verdict, p. 0763.

14. Jean-Francois Steiner, *Treblinka* (Paris, France: Librairie Artheme Fayard, 1966; English translation Simon & Schuster, Inc., 1967) p. 303.

We do not know how many of the forty survivors are alive today. Be that as it may, at least twenty-one survivors have been unable to identify John Demjanjuk as Ivan the Terrible. For its part, the Jerusalem court was prepared with five primary witnesses, had several additional witnesses in the wings, and even eventually introduced evidence by two deceased witnesses. The five primary "survivor-witnesses" were identified as Eliyahu Rosenberg (the so-called star witness, whose testimony turned out to be the most inconsistent), Pinchas Epstein, Josef Cherney (also known as Czarny), Sonia Lefkowitz and Gustav Boraks. Lefkowitz mysteriously defaulted from the trial and Borak's testimony was dismissed as incompetent.

To the best of my knowledge, no shred of evidence was ever put forth to establish that these five people were ever even incarcerated at Treblinka. Assuming that they were, however, let us regard them first in light of the Feodor Fedorenko trial which took place in Florida in 1977-78, where the foundation for the farcical Demjanjuk trial in Israel had been laid.

It seems to be a Nazi-hunter custom to use a coterie of witnesses who travel together to so-called war criminal trials during which time they socialize, reminisce, compare notes and, in effect, become a team. As they go on these excursions, their stories tend to jell in the fashion of group psychology, and they become "professional" witnesses to be used as ace weapons for the prosecution. In reality, just the opposite happens: the "witnesses" are tripped up easily by defense counsel; they forget what they are talking about; they contradict each other; they make bizarre declarations; and they attempt to neutralize their blunders by screaming about atrocities.

As an example of this unseemly behavior, one of these "witnesses" at the Fedorenko trial, Eugene Turowski, now deceased, went so far as to identify an American spectator sitting in the rear of the courtroom as a Nazi guard rather than Fedorenko himself who was sitting right across from him. Fed up, the judge threw him and the eleven other witnesses out of court and sent them packing back to Israel. Three of these "witnesses" who had appeared at the Fedorenko trial were later called in to testify against Demjanjuk.

Another disturbing aspect of the Fedorenko trial was a psychological ploy that alone should have invalidated the so-called photo identification. When a long row of small photographs was spread out for the witnesses in Florida, those of Demjanjuk and Fedorenko were unusually large, a tactic that was bound to make Fedorenko and, eventually, Demjanjuk remain in the minds of the witnesses.

Two of the witnesses who re-emerged from the Fedorenko trial, Eliyahu

Rosenberg and Pinchas Epstein, had also appeared at a war crimes trial in Dusseldorf during 1964-65, where the German prosecutor declared that they "lied like hell" and had their testimony thrown out. One would assume that once a person has been established as a liar, he can never again be called as a witness. But this evidently is not the case in Israel.

To compensate for the missing Sonia Lefkowitz, Judge Levin called on prosecution witness Miriam Radivker, aka Radiwker and Radiwoker, eighty-one, whom he identified as "a former investigator at the Nazi Crime Investigation Unit of the Israeli Police." She herself was not a Treblinka survivor but rather a key interrogator of witnesses for the prosecution. Although Mrs. Radivker gave a lengthy discourse on her history in police work, including her investigative skills and abilities, her amateurish techniques and obvious attempts to manipulate witnesses would establish her as little more than a police matron. As an example of her lack of credibility, it was shown that she gave false testimony at the 1978 Fedorenko trial in Florida when she said that the late Eugene Turowski had positively identified Demjanjuk as Ivan the Terrible. Furthermore, when Dov Levin asked Radivker during Demjanjuk's trial if she had mentioned the names of Demjanjuk and Fedorenko when questioning the witnesses, she replied in the affirmative. "This violation of accepted legal procedure came to light on Thursday, March 15 during cross-examination of the witness conducted by defense attorney Yoram Sheftel." And regarding her participation in US. court proceedings, attorney O'Connor "also read into the record a Florida judge's statements that Mrs. Radivker had engaged in *coaching* and *leading witnesses*. . . "[15] But the three Israeli judges refused to accept the Florida judgment because "it developed conclusions that could affect the John Demjanjuk trial." Radivker fervently believed that John Demjanjuk, the man she called Ivan, was stationed at Camp Sobibor, which would conform to the forged I.D. card. However, she was shocked when Turowski insisted that Ivan was at Treblinka, not Sobibor, and again when other witnesses made the same assertion. If it could be proven that Demjanjuk was never at Sobibor, then he could be cleared.

In spite of the confusion, Levin declared:

> *We were much impressed by her [Radivker's] reliability and her prodigious memory in spite of her advanced age. It is discernible that she endeavors to be exact in her description of things, that her replies are sincere and truthful and that the events from the time of her work on this subject in the year 1976 are well and clearly engraved in her*

15. The *Ukrainian Weekly*, March 22, 1987. (emphasis added)

memory. We definitely rely on her words, which are confirmed in the statements which have been taken down from the words of Turowski [sic] and one can on the basis of her words adopt the facts as described above. This we state even after having heard the numerous reservations and the sharp criticism of counsel Sheftel about the testimony of Mrs. Radiwoker and its credibility. We repudiate these reservations as groundless. [16]

Investigator Radivker had also taken a statement from Eliyahu Rosenberg on May 11, 1976, after he had reviewed a photo lineup. At that time, Rosenberg declared, "I refuse to say that I can identify him [Demjanjuk] with certainty."[17] However, at the Demjanjuk trial, Rosenberg surprisingly changed his mind: "Madam, this man, this face is known to me from Treblinka."[18] Radivker then attempted to force Rosenberg to say that Ivan was at Sobibor, not Treblinka, but Rosenberg refused. If he saw Ivan alive, Rosenberg continued, he thought he would be able to identify him even now. Rosenberg also claimed to have entered Israel on Rosh Hashana in 1942. But how could he have then been at Treblinka at the same time?

Eliyahu Rosenberg is a short, bullnecked man who appears to be intensely preoccupied. He indulged in loud outbursts and wild exaggerations, such as once declaring that three to four hundred people were shoved into a gas chamber that measured twelve by twelve feet. Even if they were standing on each others' heads, it is difficult to visualize such a scene. Instead it conjures up a vision of people endlessly climbing out of a Volkswagen or a telephone booth, the opposite reaction to what should be seen as an event of tragic proportions.

When Rosenberg was asked to walk over to Demjanjuk in order to identify him, he asked John to remove his glasses. John did so, at the same time offering a handshake. At this, Rosenberg flew into a hysterical rage, screaming that he was indeed the murderer and furious that John dared to offer his hand. Shouting that he could never forget those murderous gray eyes and that his "memories are dripping with blood . . . this open wound is enough for me," this sensational outburst caused Rosenberg's wife to faint in the courtroom.[19]

Rosenberg also claimed that he had buried bodies and had them thrown into an incinerator. But how could he do this simultaneously? (During my trip to

16. Verdict, p. 0279-80.
17. Verdict, p. 0295.
18. Verdict, p. 0297.
19. *The Buffalo News,* February 26, 1987.

Treblinka I never saw nor heard of an "incinerator," only one solitary burning pit.) And considering the grueling job of running corpses from the gas chambers to the burial pits, supposedly for eleven months, how did Rosenberg himself escape death after becoming exhausted, as he claimed. This was after all, the time when the Nazis supposedly shot the "Work-Jews"[20] in order to make room for fresh workers.

As a further illustration of the questionable reliability of his testimony, Rosenberg stated emotionally that in 1942 he had dragged the remains of his two sisters from the Treblinka gas chambers; yet in December 1945 and December 1947, Rosenberg had made statements of his wartime experiences for both the Jewish Historical Institute in Warsaw and for the Jewish Documentation Center in Vienna, but never even mentioned this appalling personal tragedy in those statements. Furthermore, Rosenberg is alleged to have testified in 1987 that he had pulled the bodies of his three daughters from the gas chambers in September 1942. But he was seventeen-and-a-half years old at the time.[21]

In December 1947, this same Rosenberg had testified before Tuvia Friedman, Chief of the Holocaust Documentation Center in Haifa (and whom Rosenberg challenged and threatened to kill after he did his about-face later), that Ivan the Terrible had been killed in the Treblinka uprising of August 1943. Giving a colorful description of Ivan's demise, he said that a group of Jewish men had rushed the barracks where the notorious guard was sleeping and proceeded to kill him. In Rosenberg's sixty-eight page statement describing the August 1943 prisoner uprising at Treblinka, handwritten in Yiddish, the *Ukrainian Weekly* quotes his assertion: "Afterwards we broke into Ivan's machine room. He was asleep at the time. Gustav hit him in the head with a spade, leaving him lying there for all eternity."[22]

The Nazis, in line with their politically orchestrated disdain of Jews, categorized the death camp inmates according to their functions, e.g , "Court-Jews" were charged with the upkeep of the camp; "Gold-Jews" sorted gold, money, jewels and other valuables taken from the prisoners; "Jews of the Square" sorted the confiscated clothing; "Jews of Death" handled the bodies, etc.

The *Cleveland Plain Dealer* ran an article stating that Edward Nishnic , Demjanjuk's son-in-law and chief fund raiser, visited the Jewish Historical Institute in Warsaw, located and copied another statement made by Eliyahu

---

20. Treblinka, Jean-Francois Steiner, p. 72.
21. *The Reporter,* Warsaw, Poland, April-May 1988, p. 23.
22. *The Ukrainian Weekly,* January 31, 1988.

Rosenberg in 1947 which revealed that Rosenberg himself " either participated in or witnessed the slaying of Ivan the Terrible at Treblinka camp in Poland." The main thrust of the article was that " Rosenberg himself either killed Ivan of Treblinka or was there when others did." Specifically, the story relates that Rosenberg and a fellow inmate known as Gustav broke into the guards barracks and "then I (or we) smacked Ivan over the head, behind the ear, so that he lay there, dead. The document, in Yiddish, is unclear whether the word he wrote was "I" or "we." Rosenberg made and signed this obviously exculpatory 1947 statement and admitted at the Demjanjuk trial that he had signed each of the eight pages of the deposition that detailed the assassination of Ivan by the inmates Subsequently, he hedged his testimony by stating that the "murder of Ivan was based on what other inmates had told him in the forest after the breakout."[23]

In 1947, two years after the calamitous World War II, one wonders how this poor ex-KZ inmate secured the financial resources to travel to Haifa and Vienna as well as his upkeep to make his depositions. One wonders about a possibly self-serving element as well as the existence of a financial backer. Furthermore, one wonders at Rosenberg's motivation to make such outlandish statements in two different, widely separated locales. And above all, one marvels at the adeptness of the judges in accepting Rosenberg's verbal turnabout in the face of his signed depositions, an act that in the United States would call for his immediate dismissal, and possibly a mistrial.

The next "redoubtable" witness from the Fedorenko trial to re-emerge in the 1987 Israeli court was Pinchas Epstein. To the rear and right of the three judges, there was displayed a large, technical map of Treblinka. O'Connor pointed to this map and asked Epstein where the victims removed their clothing before going to the one hundred-meter "slough," the fenced-in pathway to the gas chambers. Epstein was unable to locate the area on the map. O'Connor then asked Epstein about the burial pits and their locations since it was Epstein's supposed duty to escort people to pits where they would be shot. But he replied that there was just a single pit surrounded by trees which eventually died. Although Epstein apparently spent his entire stay at Treblinka in the killing area, one must ask, while a constant cycle of "arrival to undressing to death" was occurring, how Epstein, enduring many beatings and fatal markings, escaped extermination himself? Any injury ranging from a bruise to a smashed head was a fatal "marking" and called for immediate execution.

But Levin coddled Epstein to an extraordinary degree, saying that "Epstein is a reliable and careful person, and will not concoct an identification. If any

---

23. *The Cleveland Plain Dealer,* January 23, 1988.

doubt about it exists in his heart, he will say so."[24] Referring to Epstein's photo identification, Levin stated: "The difference in the picture identified by Epstein as Ivan from the rest of the pictures is that in this picture the image is missing a forelock. . . prima facie [evidence] without any doubt."[25] Such solicitous concern and conclusions from a supposedly neutral judge are highly questionable.

When Demjanjuk was shown leaving the plane upon his arrival in Israel, Epstein observed him on television and noted a supposed limping gait similar to that of Ivan of Treblinka. The chief judge saw this as a "high standard" identification. It was natural, after all, that Epstein would recognize Demjanjuk's gait since he had seen him many times on television and at the Cleveland trial. In the United States, this admission might have disqualified Epstein as a witness given that we now have the spectacle of defendants appearing in courtrooms with bags over their heads to prevent premature and erroneous identification.

In a 1960 deposition, Epstein had stated that Ivan's assistant, a man he called Nikolai, did not wear a black uniform. At the present trial, he affirmed that Nikolai *did* wear a black uniform, and that someone had "altered" his statement. Epstein also could not remember who operated the death-dealing machinery at Treblinka: Ivan, Nikolai or someone called Fritz Schmidt. Epstein also stated that he learned the identity of his brother's killer at Treblinka one hour after the murder, but at another trial he said he learned this fact one hour before the trial began.

O'Connor scored a great success when he was able to disclose glaring discrepancies between these two witnesses. Epstein, for example, stated that bodies were burned only during the day, whereas Rosenberg claimed that bodies were burned night and day. The one said that prisoner assembly occurred only at night; the other that it was morning *and* night. Where Tweedledum claimed that the diesel engine was run by Fritz Schmidt, Tweedledee said it was run by someone called Szlamek. And last but not least, Epstein described two particular German guards as being so identical they might have been twins, while Rosenberg stated that their appearances were radically different.

Witness Josef Cherney, aged sixty, who entered Treblinka at age fifteen, testified that Ivan cut off the noses, ears and breasts from naked victims, and that he shot a girl dead as she tried to climb over a fence. But his testimony followed the same contradictory pattern of Epstein and Rosenberg. Nonetheless, Levin in his verdict would later refer to Cherney's "unforgettable

24. Verdict, p. 0489
25. Verdict, p. 0490

testimony."[26]

Witness Sonia Lefkowitz did not make an appearance and no reason or explanation for this decision was given, and as described earlier, Miriam Radivker was called in her place. Gustav Boraks, eighty-seven, during the course of his testimony made the incredible statement that he had traveled by train from Israel to the United States. He was dismissed. Nonetheless, Levin, conceding that Boraks "has difficulty in remembering," stated in an amazing about-face that "in spite of the distance of time, his memory was strong."[27]

After hearing the four primary witnesses, the judges then incredibly permitted testimony by two deceased witnesses to be entered into the record, Levin explaining that the use of dead witnesses is quite legitimate in that one can refer to their pre-death writings and conversations.[28] However, this testimony was to backfire. Thus, on June 7, 1961, the late Samuel Helman had given testimony to the Yad Vashem Museum in Jerusalem, declaring that "a group of rebels overpowered the Germans and killed Ivan Grojni [sic] and threw him into the incinerator and set fire to the gas chambers."[29] Levin later conceded in his verdict that "there is a lack of clarity in the testimony of Mrs. Radiwoker [Radivker] concerning the number of pictures which she showed to Hellman [Helman] and from where they were taken."[30]

However, Helman, a.k.a. Schlomo Helman, who was in Treblinka longer than any other inmate, who helped construct the gas chambers, and who had a better opportunity than any other witness to study the real Ivan at close range, was unable to identify Demjanjuk. He also described Ivan as being age thirty when John Demjanjuk would only have been twenty-two at the time. Helman further described Ivan as a "monstrous apparition" at the gas chamber entrance striking the unfortunate victims with a sword. Using sword, bayonet, whip, dagger and revolver, the real Ivan must have been a one-man demolition team. Nevertheless, the Defense saw Helman's statement as a "*clear failure to identify Ivan* by someone who ought to have known him well and therefore this statement of Hellman [sic] *disproves* all the other identifications."[31] On March 13, 1961, the late Abraham Goldfarb had testified in a sworn statement that "'Ivan' had been killed during the prisoner's revolt on August 2, 1943,"[32]

---

26. Verdict, p. 0475
27. Verdict, p. 0478
28. That dead witnesses cannot be cross-examined is obviously irrelevant.
29. Verdict, p. 0222
30. Verdict, p. 0325
31. Verdict, p. 0327 (emphasis added)
32. *The Ukrainian Weekly,* February 14, 1988.

testimony that is substantiated by records in the possession of Bar Ilan University but was dismissed by the Levin court. Amazingly, Levin, referring later in his verdict to Goldfarb, declared: "He did not identify Fedorenko even when there was a clear hint that the man in picture 17 was reputed to be Fedorenko,"[33] a striking admission that "hints" were part and parcel of the so-called identification process.

So much for the dead "prosecution witnesses." Little did the prosecution anticipate that they would, in after-life, come to the aid of John Demjanjuk.

Other witnesses who made their way into the courtroom were not as fascinating as these four live, one missing, and two dead ones. However, one surprise witness was Yehiel Reichman, a seventy-two year old millionaire who now resides in Uruguay and who made his post-war fortune in textiles. In a U.S. court appearance on March 12, 1980, Reichman "stated in writing that he recalls nothing and no one" about Treblinka. In spite of this, Judge Levin permitted him to testify. Alternately, Reichman served at Treblinka as a barber, dentist and clothing sorter, his "dental" work consisting of removing gold fillings from the teeth of corpses. Reichman stated that he escaped from Treblinka in August 1943, and hid in a bunker until January 17, 1945, when he was freed by Russian troops. Shown maps of Treblinka, Reichman was unable to explain where he lived and worked. Eventually, he selected some places, but the answers turned out to be incorrect. Since Reichman had written a book about his experiences, he was asked why he had made no mention of Ivan the Terrible, a.k.a. Ivan Grozny. Reichman responded that there was no word in Yiddish for *Grozny* (meaning "terrible" in Polish) and therefore he used the word "Satan."

During the course of his testimony, Reichman mentioned that he moved from Treblinka to Lodz, Poland, then emigrated to Uruguay in 1956 where he proceeded to set up industries there. According to his testimony, the U.S. Embassy in 1980 asked him to participate in the Treblinka trial, an odd request on the part of our State Department when it is supposedly U.S. philosophy and policy not to meddle in the affairs of other countries. Concluding his remarks, Reichman said, "Strange , the U.S. Embassy is interested in Treblinka, but not in the problems of their own citizens."[35] We also learned that before his U.S. testimony, he had been briefed by OSI Investigator Thomas Posey, who stated in his affidavit that their discussion had been in English and without a translator. But Reichman in his testimony said one of the participants in the conference

33. Verdict, p. 0481.
34. *The Ukrainian Weekly,* March 15, 1987.
35. *The Ukrainian Weekly*

was a translator since he, Reichman, did not know English and thus his court testimony was in Yiddish.[36]

Since the Demjanjuk case was and is based on the question of identification, the Israeli court saw fit to call in a number of other alleged Treblinka survivors to testify, evidently in an attempt to accumulate an incriminating amount of "evidence" to ensure John's conviction. This tactic was also to backfire. Having perused thirty photos presented by police investigator Radivker, witness Dov Freiberg was unable to make an identification. Responding to Radivker's question, witness Meir Liss said that "a Ukrainian with the name of Ivan Demjanjuk was not known to him." Witness Shimon Greenspan was explicitly asked about picture 16 (John), whom he could not identify; he would only identify picture 17, which was that of Fedorenko. Witness Arie Kudlik admitted, "I am unable to identify anyone." Witness Kalman Taigman repeated that he, also, was unable to identify anyone. The Defense repeatedly charged that Mrs. Radivkers procedures were "tainted by intimidation," but Judge Levin refused to concur.

It is our feeling that although the Israeli court was unbelievably confident with the performance of its local witnesses, it agreed with the OSI that it would be "icing on the cake" to enlist a member of the Nazi death-dealing machinery to bolster their case against John Demjanjuk. Accordingly, OSI personnel, namely George Garand, Bernard Duarty and Norman Moskovitz, made their way to West Berlin to "interview" one Otto Horn on November 14, 1979, a sure indication that the plot against John Demjanjuk had been hatching for a long time. Horn, an S.S. killer, graduated from the euthanasia program that executed his fellow Germans. He was stationed at Treblinka from October 1942 until its destruction in September 1943. He weathered one trial in Dusseldorf in 1964 "with other Nazi criminals who served in Treblinka,"[37] and it is incredible that he was exonerated, giving rise to the suspicion that a secret plea bargain was made between him and the prosecutor. At any rate, OSI affidavits were submitted in 1986 to the Jerusalem Court. The description of Otto Horn's role at Treblinka as a "wanderer and onlooker"[38] denies the well-known Germanic drive for efficiency; to tolerate an idler and loafer is just not part of the German character.

Although Ivan was accused of operating the gas engines, Horn related that a Fritz Schmidt was in charge of the killing operation while four other men, who were identified only as Munzberger, Matthes, Suchomil and Isold, operated

---

36. Verdict, p. 0362-3
37. Verdict, p 0364.
38. Verdict, p. 0366.

the engine. Later, however, the eighty-three-year-old Horn was to give full credit to Schmidt and Ivan only. In spite of Horn's protestations of his own innocence, he claimed he saw Ivan "almost constantly," indicating that Horn himself was in close proximity to the gas chamber. Despite this, he claimed that he "never saw him beat, shoot or torture prisoners."[39] This would seem to be a serious contradiction of the Israeli witnesses' testimonies

The OSI went so far as to administer photographic identification parades to Otto Horn to assure his veracity and memory recall. He was shown two sets of eight photos each, one of which was of Ivan Demjanjuk from the 1940's. Horn examined each picture at length, but was unable to identify positively any one of them. The OSI people then placed the first set of photos in a stack with Demjanjuk's photo placed on the very top and visible to Horn. The second stack contained a photo of Demjanjuk that was taken in the 1950's. After glancing at the photo of Demjanjuk that was on top of the first stack, Horn identified the photos of Demjanjuk in both sets as photos of the same person. When he continued to study the photo in the second set, Horn said that it was definitely similar to the person he knew as Ivan. From the casual word "similar," the carefully orchestrated routine then amazingly developed into a positive identification of "Ivan of Treblinka." To proclaim publicly that such an identification procedure was a legitimate test is a travesty of justice.

O'Connor rendered a brilliant cross-examination. In response to intense questioning, Horn replied limply that he had "aged a great deal in eight years" since the OSI briefing, a feeble attempt to excuse his generalized statements such as, "he resembles him [the real Ivan]" or, "I cannot today say if this is he or not; after forty-three years a person changes."[40]

In a move more appropriate for the prosecutor, Levin also used Horn's Berlin testimony that Ivan was alive and well after the August 2nd uprising, but did not mention the highly questionable meeting between Horn and the OSI team. Neither was it mentioned that Horn was shown pictures of Demjanjuk over and over again, nor that Horn did an about-face and retracted his accusations when questioned by Mark O'Connor.

Such underhanded tactics, especially those of Judge Levin constantly interjecting himself brazenly into the legal give-and-take between the prosecution and defense attorneys and particularly attacking and undermining the defense efforts, surely indicates that this was a rigged trial with a predetermined outcome. The alert and aware Israeli public seemed to confirm this when the Demjanjuk trial began. For example, hordes of people were

---

39. Verdict, p. 0374 as recorded in memorandum Nun/74.
40. Verdict, p. 0382.

standing in line at 5 a.m. waiting to enter the courtroom of the Binyenei Hau'ma Convention Center which holds over three hundred people. The disgust with the prejudiced judges was reflected in the fact that attendance eventually dwindled to about a dozen spectators. Furthermore, decent Israelis have made a point of contacting defense lawyers and defense witnesses to apologize for what was happening in their courtroom. Defense witness Nikolai Tolstoy, for example, was overwhelmed by the number of apologies and expressions of contrite attitudes.

We also note Levin's prejudicial declaration that Martin Koller a.k.a. Kolar, the investigator who succeeded Mrs. Radivker, offered testimony that was "incontestable," and then qualified his own rigid certainty by stating: "In our opinion, it is pointless and unnecessary to enter into the details of the [Defense's] censure, part of which is baseless, the other part emanating from a wrong presentation and interpretation of the facts. Even if he [Koller] erred in several cases and in describing some facts, these were not intended and central errors."[41]

If anyone said it best, it was probably former Israeli Supreme Court Justice Haim Cohn, one of Israel's most revered and beloved justices. Cohn publicly declared his willingness to defend John Demjanjuk "if only to prevent his conviction on account of the emotional atmosphere surrounding the case. . . If he were the attorney-general today he would not take the responsibility of submitting charges against Demjanjuk. . . . After forty years it was almost impossible to bring reliable testimony [from witnesses] to prove the allegations."[42]

One other person stands out, the delightful and irrepressible Tuvia Friedman, who would always begin his statements with the expression, "Gave a listen..." Friedman seems to know and is liked by everyone in Israel, yet he has had more than his share of suffering. His family was destroyed in the hell that was wartime Poland and, more recently, he lost his beloved son in a tragic swimming accident at Eilat.

Tuvia was the first Israeli to denounce the Demjanjuk trial as a sham and a blot on the name of Israel, and since he believed that the trial would be decided in and by the media, he arranged a press conference for us in Haifa where approximately twenty Israeli journalists were in attendance, a real coup for Mark O'Connor because of his brilliant and incisive responses to the Israeli newsmen. Tuvia also broadcast a radio message denouncing the spurious

41. Verdict, p. 0446.
42. *The Jerusalem Post,* November 19, 1986

accusations of the trial and issued a call for justice. For these efforts, he put up with harassment and even death threats from such persons as Eliyahu Rosenberg.

The desperate attempts to prove that John Demjanjuk was at Sobibor; the blatant change in stories by Rosenberg after he left Ivan "lying there for all eternity"; the testimony of so-called survivors who never proved that they were survivors, who continued to participate in their grisly tasks over a long period of time even though they were "marked" by bruises but were still not summarily executed as was the normal procedure, and who continued to rely on their convenient forgetfulness — all this adds up to the incompetence and unsuitability of the so-called witnesses. In the United States, they would have met the same fate as the Fedorenko witnesses and been thrown out of court or jailed for perjury.

One recalls the perceptive insight of Buffalo attorney Mark Jasen in his stern admonition to the jurors in a U.S. case: "Beware of witnesses who witnessed nothing!"[43] It is tragic that in the Demjanjuk trial, there was no jury to counterbalance the furious prejudice of a hanging judge, a judge who had the temerity to refer to the questions of the defense as "ruthless."[44]

We must also remember the Cult of the Survivors. It is a fact of life that the survivors are national, religious heroes, sanctified to sainthood simply for the act of surviving. We outlanders cannot grasp the enormity of the prestige and believability of this caste, but it is as though the end of a millennia of Jewish suffering were being celebrated with a banquet and blood-sacrifice of one single victim. And the celebration is due solely to the existence of "the survivors." Presumably, the German, Eichmann, had served that purpose, but evidently a Ukrainian or Balt was also a necessary victim to symbolize the "helpers" of the Nazis in order to satiate the lust for vengeance and revenge.

But for a detached and neutral perspective of the "witness syndrome," we refer to the succinct and wise words of Elizabeth Loftus, a psychologist and Adjunct Professor of Law at the University of Washington in Seattle, who specializes in memory and who has testified in hundreds of cases where eyewitness testimony is crucial. In view of her Jewish heritage, strong feelings about "the crime," and pressure from her family and friends, she unfortunately declined to testify at the trial. However, her brilliant exposition of the factors involved, as outlined in a *Newsweek* essay, is dazzling testimony that helps to demolish the validity of witness "evidence."

43. *The Buffalo News,* October 19, 1988
44. Verdict, p. 0382

This expert states without reservation: "I know that the human mind is subject to distortion. People often remember things differently from the way they really were. And contrary to the popular belief that traumatic events tend to create an indelible 'fixation' in the mind, such traumas are often associated with memory problems." Ms. Loftus' work has brought her in contact with "an unusual class of people - those accused of crimes they did not commit." Giving the example of wrongful accusation in a rape case, when confronted with the accused in court, the victim went into hysterics and "that helped convince everyone that he was guilty." An important truth emerged from this: "People are impressed by confident eyewitness testimony. Yet, research has shown little or no relationship between a witness' confidence and his or her accuracy of recall." It is significant that the accused, an innocent man, shortly thereafter died from a stress-caused heart attack. The insightful psychologist concluded: "But the critical issue in the Ivan case is whether the face identified by these survivors out of that sea of sadism is the right face. As a psychologist, I believe, in principle, that if there is a scientific answer to a question, it must be provided no matter who is asking the question." The most hopeful aspect of her essay is that "there is...a body of research challenging the value of eyewitness memory."[45] And, one is forced to wonder, was Dov Levin ever really interested in ascertaining whether or not the person in front of him was the real Ivan the Terrible?

A most striking observation might be that the lower court was guilty of excessive intervention in an extreme and unprecedented manner when defense witnesses were having difficulty, and the judges' questions were obviously designed to intensify their difficulty. Conversely, the lower court intervened frequently in cross-examination of prosecution witnesses, specifically to assist them in extricating themselves from a difficult situation. The court frankly assisted the Prosecution and damaged the Defense. By its persistent, unremitting help to the prosecution the court, in effect, became part of the Prosecution.

45. *Newsweek,* June 29, 1987

John Demjanjuk leaving the Israeli Courthouse Building on August 13, 1987

A sketch of the real "Ivan the Terrible" taken from eyewitness observations.

Painting of "Ivan the Terrible" at Yad Vashem museum.

A Nazi I.D. card forged by the Russians and supplied to the Israeli prosecution. This card was delivered to the Israelis by Armand Hammer.

A photo of the burning pit at the Treblinka Death Camp taken by the author.

Drawing of a Burning Pit — by S. Willenberg

Copies of two passports showing cancelled visas by U.S. Embassy in Warsaw of the two witnesses who could have testified to Demjanjuk's innocence.

OBYWATEL POLSKI
ПОЛЬСКИЙ ГРАЖДАНИН - CITOYEN POLONAIS

nazwisko i imię — **SAMUEL EUGENIA**

data urodzenia — 20. 3. 1927 r.

miejsce urodzenia — WÓLKA OKRĄGLIK

miejsce zamieszkania — WÓLKA OKRĄGLIK

RYSOPIS
ПРИМЕТЫ - SIGNALEMENT

wzrost / taille — 154 cm.

oczy / yeux — P...

znaki szczególne / signes particuliers — NI...

Podpis posiadacza

SERIA PF NR 000417

OBYWATEL POLSKI
ПОЛЬСКИЙ ГРАЖДАНИН - CITOYEN POLONAIS

nazwisko i imię — **WUJEK JÓZEF**

data urodzenia — 04.07.1925 r.

miejsce urodzenia — WÓLKA-ORĄGLIK

miejsce zamieszkania — ...

RYSOPIS
ПРИМЕТЫ - SIGNALEMENT

Podpis posiadacza

SERIA PE NR 730432

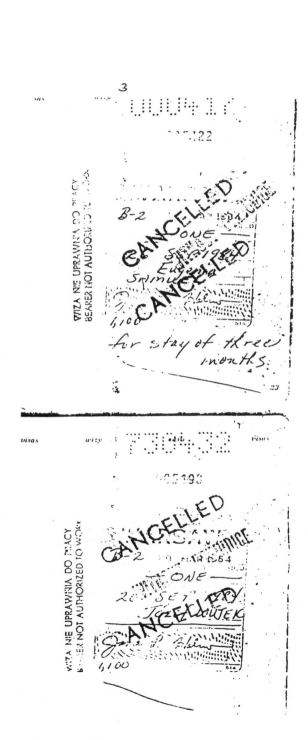

CHAPTER SEVEN – WHERE WAS THE ACCUSED?

With the exposure of the false I.D. card and the unbelievable testimony of neurotic prosecution witnesses who lacked substantive reasons to convict John Demjanjuk as Ivan the Terrible, the Jerusalem court was forced to resort to its last major argument, expressed succinctly by a former Knesset member who appeared on a national Canadian television network program and declared: "Demjanjuk is guilty because he cannot account for two years of his life." She recognized, of course, that if John had been incarcerated at the Chelm POW camp for eighteen months, he could not have been at the Treblinka or Sobibor death camps. She also added on six months to solidify her assertion.

Most people forget and repress traumatic events in their past, particularly in wartime. My own experience in the Navy during World War II is a case in point. Under constant alert and attack in the Pacific, my wartime experience remains to this day one great blur with faces, dates and places utterly forgotten. If I, as a college youth, could forget dates, places and the names of my fellow crewmen in the South Pacific, is it not understandable that John Demjanjuk, a shy youth who took eight years to complete four grades of school, and alternated using the same pair of shoes with his father, could be just as forgetful?

In reviewing the portion of the verdict that deals with John's whereabouts during that crucial time, it is most obnoxious that Levin repeatedly refers to the "lies" of John Demjanjuk, and to John as a "liar," assertions which, in our opinion, only serve to show how psychological ploys were used by a court eager to convict.

Nevertheless, Levin does make an effort to present Demjanjuk's "alibi," stating: "The accused claims that when Ivan the Terrible was committing his dreadful crimes in Treblinka, he, the accused, was a German prisoner-of-war in Poland, in a camp called Chelm (Cholem).[46] The word alibi has a bad connotation. It implies, in the courtroom, an excuse for not being found guilty. In examining records of youthful offenders on many occasions, I would often see the defense, "It's only a charge, not a conviction." Yet, the charge alone frequently casts a black cloud over the youth. Levin expounded on his own philosophy of the alibi:

46. Verdict, p. 0683.

*A claim of alibi can be a two-edged sword. When it stands up –
nothing can better it, and it proves clearly that the prosecution
witnesses are mistaken or lying; and in any case, the court will never
convict according to identification witnesses where the claim of alibi is
proven to its satisfaction. And where the claim of alibi falls – it can
sometimes strengthen the arguments of the prosecution. An alibi found
to be false serves the same ends as other lies of an accused, often
strengthening the evidence of the prosecution, giving it added
credibility and weight.*[47]

At another point , Levin declares: "If the alibi is not refuted but the accused
gives conflicting versions, this will also strengthen the evidence of the
prosecution." It is interesting that nowhere does John Demjanjuk contradict his
statement of being in Chelm for eighteen months. It is also interesting that
nowhere does Levin insist that the burden of proof is on the Prosecution to
establish that John was somewhere other than Chelm during the existence of the
Treblinka death camp.

Levin does, however, make a point of summarizing Demjanjuk's history as
John related it to the court:

*In 1942 he was drafted into the Red Army. In the summer of 1941,
war broke out between Germany and Russia, and about three months
later the accused was wounded in his back from the shrapnel of an
artillery shell. [How could he have been wounded in 1941 if he was
not drafted until 1942?] He was hospitalized in four hospitals, and
when he recovered he was transferred to an artillery unit in Kotaissi,
and from there to Baku and then to Kerch in the Crimea. In the spring
of 1942, in the battle known as the "Battle of Kerch," the accused was
taken prisoner, together with an entire army, by the Germans. For
several weeks he and other prisoners were given work by the
Germans, first burying German soldiers (protocol p. 5362), and then
narrowing railway tracks to adapt them to the width of the German
tracks; at that time the accused was living with his friends in a railway
carriage. From there he was transferred to a prisoner-of-war camp in
Rovno. He was there for only a week or two before being transferre d
to the Chelm prisoner-of-war camp.*

47. Verdict, p. 0677.

According to the accused he stayed at Chelm for eighteen months, and was engaged partly in the construction of billets, and partly in unloading coal, potatoes and swedes at the nearby railroad station. But mainly, for ten months he was engaged in cutting turf. This was extremely hard work done under very difficult conditions. Hunger and disease devastated the prisoners, and the accused himself became very thin, "skin and bones."

After about eighteen months the Germans separated several hundred Ukrainians from the rest of the prisoners and transferred them, with the accused among them, to Graz, in Austria. Prior to this transfer the prisoners-of-war received Italian uniforms in place of the rags remaining of their Russian uniforms. At that time, a Ukrainian Division in German service was being organized in Graz, and the accused was supposed to join this division. The Ukrainian prisoners were housed in a stable in Graz, and it is unclear whether they trained or did nothing. The accused's blood-type is tattooed under his left armpit.

After two or three weeks in Graz, the accused was transferred to a prisoner-of-war camp in Hoyberg [sic] Germany, and joined a Russian division in German service called the "Volsov Army," [sic] whose insignia was R.O.A., meaning Russian Liberation Army. The accused was posted to a unit whose duty was to guard the generals, and he was designated to guard – without weapons – General Truchin [sic] of the Volsov Army , but since he had no uniform he never actually did guard duty. The accused remained in Hoyberg until two or three weeks before the end of the war. From there he was transferred to Salzburg, and from there he reached Bishopshofen and fell into the hands of the American army. He and other prisoners were transferred to work on a farm near Munich, and from there to the Displaced Persons Camp in Landshot [sic]. From Landshot to Regensburg, from there to Ulm, from there to Bad Reichenhall and from there to Feldapping [sic], and from there, via the Medical Board in Stuttgard [sic] to the U.S.A.

The essence of the claim of alibi is focused on the period when the accused claims that he was at the prisoner-of-war camp in Chelm.

According to his claim and the order of events that he puts forward , his time at Chelm corresponds with the time of the activities of Ivan the Terrible at Treblinka. The defense brought no proof of this claim apart from the accused's own evidence. The entire claim of alibi is therefore dependent on the credibility of the accused, and whether he succeeded in arousing a reasonable doubt that he was indeed in Chelm throughout the relevant period.[48]

The prosecution attacked Demjanjuk's alibi "both of itself and from the historical aspect. Of itself – for the paucity of detail it contains and the multiplicity of its versions and internal contradictions, and for its unreasonability." Attempting to justify this position, the prosecution's stand is summarized:

From the historical aspect, the prosecution brought evidence...whose essence was – that if the accused was in Chelm for eighteen months, he could not have met the Ukrainian division in Graz at that time, nor the Volsov Army, as these armies came into being only much later.[49]

Prior to repeating Demjanjuks reprise of his suffering at Chelm, Levin condensed the charge against him to its basics:

According to the prosecution, the accused arrived at the Trevniki [sic] camp no later than July 19, 1942, after which he perpetrated the crimes of which he is accused at Treblinka from October 1942 until the end of the extermination at Treblinka in the fall of 1943 (and in the meantime served some time, from March 27, 1943, at Sobibor).[50]

After reference was made to Demjanjuk's two trials in the United States, one for revocation of citizenship and one for deportation, Levin stated that Demjanjuk had testified to a U.S. investigator named Ziplona on April 20, 1978, that he was only in two camps in Poland: "the first was Ronovo [sic] and the second he does not remember."[50] He did, however, remember building huts in the second camp. Continuing, Levin declared:

48. Verdict, p. 0684
49. Verdict, p. 0686

The accused first mentions the Chelm camp by name in his reply to the questionnaire given to him in the U.S.A. and presented to the court on December 3, 1979 (Exhibit 191/T, p. 13, answer 26 (e) (Incidentally, it is here also that the name of Graz, Hoyberg and Bishopshofen first appear, which he had not mentioned in his investigation by Ziplona). In question 42 (p. 20) of 191/T, the accused was asked to cite the names of the places and type of work and tasks he did while a prisoner-of-war, and he replied: "Russia – laying of railway tracks. Poland – (Chelm) building huts."[50]

Israeli State Attorney Yona Blattman was aghast that Demjanjuk forgot to name Chelm and the hard labor of cutting turf under terrible conditions. He felt that such forgetfulness was surprising since Demjanjuk could remember other places where he spent a relatively short time. But he does not take into account that people normally fill out questionnaires in a brief and abrupt manner, seeing it as a tedious task to be finished as soon as possible.

Defense witness Willem A. Wagenaar[51] addressed Blattman's concerns and Judge Levin summarized his remarks as well as including his own remarks:

Forgetting the name of the camp – it is possible that the accused never knew the name of the Chelm camp. Chelm is the name of the town, while the camp was perhaps known as 'Stalag 370' (Photograph 319) or some similar name. And if the accused did not know the name, it is not surprising that he could not name it.

Also, if the accused was in many prisoner-of-war camps, with each camp, each entry and exit similar to the other, it is possible that some of them became confused one with another and his memory of the Chelm camp was covered by his memory of other camps. It is not that the memory of his camp was obliterated, he simply forgot to mention it in his life history.

This is the explanation given by Professor Wachnar [sic] in his direct examination. When he was cross-examined by the Deputy State Attorney, Mr. Shaked, the witness offered a new explanation for the accused's forgetting the suffering he underwent at the camp. The explanation is that the accused's difficult childhood experiences, at the time of the great famine in the Ukraine, and his war experiences and his being seriously wounded, all hardened his mind until he was impervious to the cutting of turf at Chelm, which did not make an impression on him strong enough to remain in his mind (Protocol pp. 7795-7807). Since his entire life had been a difficult one, the sufferings of captivity and cutting turf were not unusual enough to stand out in his memory. And if the prosecutor sees hard labor under terrible conditions as an unusual experience, the witness says: "I see it as something belonging to his normal way of life . . . the mold of his normal life were not of the most pleasant. . . the difference was not so great." (Protocol p. 7803).[52]

But Judge Levin's reaction was merely to state: "Out of respect for Professor Wagenaar we will say only this, that these explanations have no basis."[53]

It was also stated in court that Demjanjuk forgot his post-war service with the International Refugee Organization (IRO) police unit with whom he had served at Landshut, Germany, for almost a year, a fact that is significant in establishing Demjanjuk's inability to organize his memory's priorities. Again, the judge was negative, rejecting Wagenaar's testimony as "baseless assumptions," adding that "this one-dimensional scantiness and lack of all verisimilitude also indicate that this is a fabricated version."[54]

The court then called upon several historians to prove that the alibi of the accused was historically impossible. One of the "experts" even ventured the incredible opinion that Germany and Poland were allies during World War II. Levin, acting as his own historian, stated in his verdict that when Demjanjuk was taken captive, he was taken to the Rovno POW camp, and after a period there, was transferred to Chelm where he supposedly remained for eighteen months. From there, he made his way to Graz where he found the Second Ukrainian Division of General Shandruk. After several weeks, he was then posted to a unit in the Vlasov Army. But according to this chronology, it was unreasonable that after his eighteen months at Chelm, Demjanjuk found army units at Graz and Heuberg that did not come into being until almost a year later.

Demjanjuk could very well have erred in using the figure of eighteen months, and that he could have been at Chelm considerably longer. Also,

---

51. Willem A. Wagenaar is Professor of Experimental Psychology, Leiden University, the Netherlands. He is a distinguished psychologist and authority on forensic identification, has vast experience, and testified as an expert witness for the defense in this trial.

52. Verdict, p. 0690

53. Verdict, p. 0692.

54. Verdict, p. 0695.

according to the testimony of Count Nikolai Tolstoy, chaos prevailed in Germany in 1944 and there were various units and groups of the Osttrupen in Germany, thousands of whom wore the Russian Liberation Army (ROA) tag a long time before the organization of Vlasov's divisions. As proof, the court was shown photos of Vlasov men wearing the ROA tag in 1943. Tolstoy also stated that "the movements of masses should not be compared to the fate of the individual, and it is possible that individuals or small, scattered units were on the move without this being recorded in the history books. It is therefore not impossible that in April 1944 there were Osttrupen wearing the ROA tag in Hoyberg and it is them that the accused met."[55]

Since some of the events described in this book occurred so long ago, it is important to discuss the Vlasov Army — a real fighting unit and not a guard unit — because of John Demjanjuk's membership in it. Especially important is Count Tolstoy's assertion that the records of a Vlasovite Colonel Kromiadi "goes far to bear out Demjanjuk's story." The German military unfortunately styled Vlasov formations as "guard units" in spite of the fact that they were really combat units. Subsequently, Count Tolstoy advised us that "Kromiadi's unit was formally styled a 'guard' unit though it had no specific duties connected with the appellation . . .when Demjanjuk was told at Heuberg that he was a 'guard,' it may have meant no more than that he was officially attached to this or a similarly-named unit."[56]

Kromiadi's Russian-language autobiography, as well as Tolstoy's commentary, is in the hands of defense attorney Sheftel in Israel. To the best of our knowledge, this vitally important material was never utilized in the trial. In our own research to establish that the Vlasovites were a fighting force, we note the remarks of German soldier and author Jurgen Thorwald:

Zykov saw the possibility of bringing the whole idea of Russian liberation right out into the open. Tresckow and his Ic, Gersdorff, in their impatience hit on the idea of establishing a kind of model brigade as a sample of what a Russian liberation army could be. The brigade would be entirely under Russian leadership, would wear altered Russian uniforms, would be provided with Russian weapons, and would have only a small German liaison staff.

As the nucleus for this brigade, to which they gave the name 'Experimental Formation Center,' they selected the remnants of a

---

55. Verdict, p. 0717
56. Letter dated August 17, 1988 from Count Tolstoy to this writer.

*somewhat mysterious military unit that had been set up in March,
1942 by the Abwehr (German Army Counterintelligence). The
formation had been housed in a barracks camp formerly belonging to
the Soviet peat works of Ossintorf.*

*In conjunction with Abwehr Squad 203 in Smolensk, a number of
Russian exile officers, including ex-Colonel Konstantin Kromiadi,
Second Lieutenant Igor Zakharov (who had fought in Spain under
General Franco), Lieutenant Grigory Lamsdorff (a count), and several
others from prison camps had set up a 'Russian Brigade for Special
Missions.' This undertaking was also known as Operation Grayhead.*

*Its mission was commando operations behind the Soviet front. The
strength of the unit at times reached 7000 men, with four battalions
and an artillery regiment. Equipment consisted of captured weapons.
The uniforms were Russian, but were distinguished by different
epaulets and white-blue-red cockades. Kromiadi, who used the alias
'Sanin,' sometimes gave his formation the romantic-sounding name
RNNA, standing for 'Russian National People's Army.'[57]*

Levin touches on Demjanjuk's listing of Sobibor as one of his places of
residence. John's version is that a United Nations Relief and Rehabilitation
Administration (UNRRA) official warned the DPs of an impending visit by the
dreaded Soviet repatriation commission, and strongly recommended that they
select a town in Poland or Czechoslovakia to indicate past residences.
Demjanjuk's belief, after perusing a map, was that he selected Sambor, not
Sobibor, as a former residence, and that the official misunderstood him. This
explanation is reinforced by the fact that Demjanjuk could not at the time read
Roman script nor was he a good map reader. The court correctly related that
displaced persons' applications for assistance and emigration were meticulously
and thoroughly investigated, which would indicate that if a person were really
stationed at a death camp, the DP Commission Case Analyst would have been
aware of it, and subsequently would have rejected the application for
emigration.

It is interesting that the court offered a hypothetical, "sincere" defense for
Demjanjuk in speculating on the fact that if only he had been stationed at Camp

57. Jurgen Thorwald, *The Illusion,* (New York, N.Y.: Harcourt Brace Jovanovich,
1974-75) p. 96. (emphasis added)

Sobibor — which would be in agreement with the forged I.D. card — this would expunge his guilt of having served at Treblinka. But the court tempered its concern by theorizing that Demjanjuk "denies this alibi only because he is forced to" because of his version of residential history in the U.S., "and therefore the court must carry out for him by 'open the mouth of the lamb.'"[58] The meaning of this expression is unclear but it would appear that the court would just as assuredly convict John for being at the Sobibor death camp as at Treblinka. In his rambling narration, Levin said:

> *We already stated above that the assumption that the defendant was only at Sobibor, requires an additional assumption that there was a man in Treblinka who was so similar to him [John] that all the identifying witnesses mistook him for him. And that he is so similar to him in name and appearance and height and age and facial features and the shape of the ears and baldness at such an early age and in his duties. This assumption is so far-fetched that it cannot be believed at all.*

> *When the survivors speak of Ivan the Terrible being in Treblinka "all the time" and "until the end" it must be understood against the background of the "other planet" of Treblinka, in which the time dimension was so different from the ordinary human conception.[59]*

But why keep coming back to this possibility? There is a rumor to the effect that maybe there was such a man, a very cruel man, named "Demjanak," who was the real culprit. For example, Levin called on the ghost of Feodor Fedorenko, a man who had served about a year in Treblinka but was able to conceal this in his application for emigration. Simultaneously, he placed himself in a small and relatively unknown KZ camp in which he served as well. The supposedly neutral Levin then makes the absurd charge that "it is the same situation with Demjanjuk." But this analogy is unacceptable because Fedorenko was a completely different man with a completely different history. In fact, there was an air of mystery about him: After emigrating to America, he was permitted to return to the USSR as a tourist, unbelievable permission for that era, and even live there for awhile. But eventually, the Soviets executed him. As "clarified" in the verdict:

58. Verdict, p. 0746
59. Verdict, p. 0749-50.

> *It had been proven before us that the war criminal Fiudor [sic]*
> *Fedorenko, a Russian soldier, after taken prisoner by the Germans,*
> *acted as Wachman at Treblinka and after the war emigrated to the*
> *USA, visited the U.S.S.R., his home town in Ukraine with an American*
> *passport three times during 1972 for three weeks, in 1973 for thre e*
> *months and during 1975-1976 for twelve months (the questionnaire*
> *T/209 and the preliminary of Fedorenko T/2ii). . . .*

> *During all these period [sic] he was not harmed by anyone, he came*
> *and went to the U.S.S.R. freely and proceedings were taken against*
> *him only after he had been extradited by the Americans after it had*
> *been determined in judicial procedures that he was a Treblinka man. .*
> *. . [60]*

It was alleged to us that the OSI, usually servile in its relationship with the KGB, did insist to their Russian counterpart on the execution of Fedorenko. What other explanation is there in view of Fedorenko's frequent visits to the USSR under harmonious conditions, and then a sudden and unexpected carrying out of the death penalty? We also wonder why the name Fedorenko was introduced so frequently in the Demjanjuk trial. The judge's motive evidently was to identify Fedorenko's history as a duplication of or as a similar circumstance to that attributed to John Demjanjuk.

There is also the testimony of Rachel Miller,[61] an elderly lady from Boston, who called us one day to express her outrage over a story that had appeared in the *Boston Herald* which was accompanied by a photograph of John Demjanjuk and alleging that he might be "Ivan the Terrible of Treblinka." She termed the article a lie and asked that we send someone to Boston to meet with her for her story. As principal investigator, I made arrangements to meet with her and we established an immediate rapport

From her own tragic history in war-torn Europe, she had three friends who had known the real Ivan the Terrible. She identified them as Vanja Ribalka, Dimitru Wisnovsky and Ivan Filipovic, and said Ivan's real name was Vanja Ivan *Demjanak*. In a statement that she gave to me, she said that she had many discussions with these men, allegedly Ivan's best friends, regarding him and that she was shown photographs of the real Ivan on many occasions. She further

---

60. Verdict, p. 0589-90.
61. A pseudonym to protect her identity. Mrs. Miller, a former refugee, was imprisoned and tortured in four Nazi camps. Her husband, a high government official, and children were executed for helping refugees escape. In spite of her age and infirmities, she accompanied me to a Boston artist to sketch a picture of the real Ivan.

declared that:

> *Demjanak's face and likeness is firmly registered in my mind. He and Demjanjuk are definitely not the same man. Ribalka, Wisnovsky and Filipovic were not guards at Treblinka and, to the best of my knowledge, they now reside in Yugoslavia, Romania or Switzerland. They are unaware of the final fate of the real Ivan. They did attest to me that originally Ivan was a "nice human" person who was torture d by the German-Nazis, and driven to the point of madness. Obviously, the real Ivan would have to be crazed, demented and deranged to perpetrate such abominable cruelties on his fellow human beings.*

> *Should Israel execute or imprison an innocent man to symbolize the insanity of the Holocaust and as a seeming education device to pervert its youth, Israel herself would degenerate to the level of the Nazi S.S. and blackguards and be a worse curse to the world community and all mankind.*

Mrs. Miller also stated that Demjanak was about thirty-eight which would make him much older than the twenty-two-year-old Demjanjuk, and said that the real Ivan had a birthmark in the shape of a toad on his left upper underarm which made him the subject of merciless kidding and ridicule from his peers. If John were the real Ivan, he would have had this birthmark removed, a fact that could be easily ascertained by medical specialists.

Something that cannot be emphasized strongly enough is that the Jerusalem court chose to ignore the fact that thousands of other Ukrainians have an appearance similar to John Demjanjuk. Even in the United States, this writer has observed many men strikingly similar to John, i.e., short neck, husky build, round face, etc. A jurist once said that "mistaken identification is a frequent occurrence and such testimony should not be depended on." One of the most offensive aspects of the so-called identification procedures of this trial is the fact that the OSI deliberately withheld information on Treblinka inmates who were not able to identify John Demjanjuk as the sadistic guard. In addition to observing that the OSI investigators broke every rule pertaining to photo identification, one wonders why these super-efficient sleuths never bothered to administer Rorschach or polygraph tests on their victims. Perhaps they are enamored of the Napoleonic Code wherein a person is automatically guilty until he can prove his innocence.

CHAPTER EIGHT – THE DEFENSE REACTS

Although the supposedly neutral Judge Levin exhibited regard and concern for the prosecution witnesses, he expressed only disdain and even animosity for the defense witnesses, including documentation experts Julius Grant from England, Willem Wagenaar of Holland, William Flynn and Edna Robertson of the United States and, above all, Count Nikolai Tolstoy of England.

Defense witness Avraham Shifrin, discharged as a Captain in the Red Army in 1945, was subsequently sentenced to twenty-five years imprisonment after being falsely accused of being a spy for the United States. The sentence was reduced to ten years in Siberia and he eventually made his way to Israel where he is regarded as an expert on the KGB. He is active in national movements of different peoples, especially Ukrainians, who seek to be free of the Soviets and Communism. As an expert, Shifrin testified that the KGB routinely creates forged files against so-called deserters from the USSR. He further testified that there is a special department of the KGB dealing with forgeries, which utilizes authentic documents from all over the world for the purpose of these forgeries. In his historical appraisal, Shifrin emphasized that the Soviets want to fight the National Ukrainian movement by hurting the defendant and creating conflict between Jews and Ukrainians in Western countries. Levin felt that this assertion did not hold up "in the test of logic."[62] Yet, it is accepted that the Soviets have a tremendous fear of any of their citizens who have seen life in the West, and their chief target historically has been the Ukrainians.

For many years, perhaps centuries, there has been bad feeling between Jews and Ukrainians, and this hostility has followed along to wherever these ethnic groups have emigrated. For example, in response to a letter to the Knesset dated September 18, 1986, from Ms. Bozhena Olshaniwsky, President of Americans for Human Rights in Ukraine, expressing concern over the unreasonably long detention of John Demjanjuk without charges being brought against him and the intensification of accusatory charges made by Israeli government representatives, she received a reply dated October 1986 from Dov B. Ben-Meir, Deputy Speaker of the Knesset, whose letter concludes:

---

62 Verdict, p. 0589

All along the years of the Nazi occupation of the Ukraine, uncounted numbers of your compatriots collaborated with the Nazi regime, especially in the annihilation of hundreds of thousands of Jews. After the German defeat, part of these collaborators fled to the West and also escaped to the U.S.A.

During more than four decades, not a single word was heard from your organization in favor of the human rights of Ukrainians of the Jewish faith who were shot, burned, gassed by your fellow countrymen. And it is only the "worry" whether the Israeli press will by its publicity prejudice the objectivity of Israeli justice, that keeps you awake at night!

I can reassure you: Israeli justice will hold fair judgement!

To you and your friends, I suggest that you go to church not only on Sunday but also every day of the week, and that you kneel there until bleeding at the knees *in asking forgiveness for what your people has done to ours.*

With such vitriolic hatred for Ukrainians, was it possible for John Demjanjuk to get a fair trial in such an atmosphere? And did Israel try John Demjanjuk, or the Ukrainian nation?

Count Nikolai Tolstoy made a brilliant presentation in exposing Soviet Procurator Roman Rudenko as a liar and forger in his involvement in this case and with the OSI. Rudenko, as prosecutor in USSR trials of the 1930s , "admitted to Khrushchev that the admissions were extorted from the people under duration and pressure. . . and it is also known that in those trials use was made of forged documents."[63] At the Nuremberg war trials, Rudenko tried to blame the Germans with the murder of a minor, "basing himself on forced documents."[63] After heated objections by the British and American judges, he withdrew his attempt. The reprehensible, amoral conduct of Rudenko must, by definition, cast a grave shadow over the cooperation of the OSI and KGB, and the international messenger, Armand Hammer

Levin, as expected in the light of the rest of his conduct, dismissed these serious implications by declaring, ". . . even if that man [Rudenko] was involved, in past years in forgery of documents. . . the document [I.D. card] was

---

63. Verdict, p. 0585.

passed on by [him] by virtue of his holding the office of State Attorney."[64] The office evidently sanctifies the culprit. The judge then makes a remarkable concession which we paraphrase: "The USSR is an important source, the only one, for that matter, for Nazi documents and it is a closed country where there is no access to the archives."[65] Yet, we are supposed to buy the authenticity of their so-called legitimate documentation?

Levin's slashing attack on Tolstoy as a man "whose hatred of the regime in the Soviet Union on the one hand, and his sympathy for the Ukrainians and Cossacks on the other hand, have confused him and the objectivity for which every serious researcher should strive" was astonishing.[66]

But do Tolstoy's remarks really disqualify him? Tolstoy's position is that "the crimes of the Soviet regime were much more serious than Nazi crimes, and the latter should not be persecuted if justice is not administered to the former."[67] The murder of an estimated 60 million people ascribed to the Soviet Union during its relatively short history is indeed a grim matter, one regarded with horror by civilized people. No less a democracy than Canada has taken the same perspective as Tolstoy. In fact, we believe that Tolstoy's contribution was so vital that it helped to influence Canada to make two important and realistic decisions: that war crime trials, including punishment where indicated, be held entirely on Canadian soil, and that war criminals of all nationalities be investigated.

Other distinguished members of the defense, either as witnesses or as part of the legal defense team, made important contributions to Demjanjuk's case, some of whom have already been mentioned. Julius Grant of Great Britain, one of the world's foremost document examiners and who had exposed the forged Adolf Hitler diaries, played an important role in destroying as legitimate evidence the Trawniki identity card.[68] Willem Wagenaar, Dean of the Faculty of Social Sciences at the University of Leiden, Holland, manifested through defense counsel Yoram Sheftel that the manner of showing witnesses a photo-spread, as done in Demjanjuk's case, "is not a test of memory, but a manipulation, a bending of the memory." Wagenaar, an experimental psychologist, had done many tests with his students and colleagues which established that such an identity parade could become a "charade." He also emphasized that "visual memory can lose detail over the years."[69]

64. Verdict, p. 0586.
65. Verdict, p. 0588
66. Verdict, p. 0732
67. Verdict, p. 0733
68. *The Cleveland Plain Dealer,* November 11, 1987
69. *The Jerusalem Post,* November 28,1987

Professor Yasser Iscan, an American forensic anthropologist, in response to a long and wearying grilling by Prosecutor Michael Shaked, made the interesting observation that the prosecutor "can fix questions and conditions in so many ways, so that Mr. Shaked finally gets the answer he wants."[70]

Defense attorney John Gill recalled a day he left documents at Ayalon for his client to read. When he returned the following day, Demjanjuk said: "It was too hot to read them. We'll do it later." This episode and others inspired Gill to describe John Demjanjuk as "a country bumpkin kind of guy. . . he's. . . childlike. . . a fantastically unusual situation."[71]

Lead defense attorney Yoram Sheftel, angry and frustrated, frequently attacked the court, but to no avail. He was especially annoyed that the judges tolerated the "haughty and flippant behavior of Miriam Radiwker." Sheftel charged that "95% of the time the judges disallow the defense's questions. . . the judges frequently interrupt the defense, stating that its questions are a waste of time. . . and they tolerate constant commotion in the courtroom." In a highlight of the trial, Sheftel repeatedly referred to the hostility of the judges and asked them to disqualify themselves. The request was rejected."[72]

In a *Spotlight* story regarding the procurement of the so-called original Trawniki identity card by Armand Hammer, author Alec de Montmorency identified the Russian-language Israeli newspaper that broke the story as *Nasha Strana*. Remarkably, this newspaper and *Maa'riv,* as Israeli paper, both established that John Demjanjuk was handed over to Israel by the U.S. illegally:

> *During the extradition procedure, international legal norms, which stipulate the establishment of primary identity of the subject accused of crimes, were rudely violated. In reality, as it is now evident, Demjanjuk was handed over to Israel without the establishment of his identity because the United States did not have in its possession a single document (as well as not a single witness deposition) which established the identity of Demjanjuk as the so-called Ivan the Terrible. The only document which could be included in the proceeding was received by Israel in December of 1986, nine months after the decision by the United States to deport him to the Middle Eastern ministate.*

70. *The Jerusalem Post,* January 2, 1988
71. *The Cleveland Plain Dealer,* August 2, 1987
72. *Ukrainian Weekly,* March 29, 1987

In an accompanying article, Executive Editor Fred Blahut wrote:

> *Despite the total lack of credible evidence, the OSI presented its
> dramatic 'Ivan the Terrible' case to the U.S. District Court in
> Cleveland. The fundamental contradictions in time, place and person
> between the original Soviet charge of 'anti-Soviet treason' and the
> subsequent monumental genocide/war crimes charges of the Israeli
> 'eyewitnesses' were conveniently disposed of by the OSI by simply
> waiving all of the Soviet charges during presentation of the
> government's case, yet keeping the official-looking 'Nazi ID card in
> the record to add weight to its case.*[73]

To the best of my knowledge, this matter was never even brought up during
the trial.

It is disturbing that many exonerating statements and admissions never
found their way into the Israeli courtroom. As another example, Kurt Franz,
former Commandant of the Treblinka Death Camp and who is now confined in
a German prison, could of all people be expected to know his entire staff,
German or Ukrainian. But after seeing John Demjanjuk on television in his
cell, he declared without reservation: "I do not know this man; I have never
seen this man ; there was an Ivan in my camp, but this is not he [Demjanjuk] "[74]

There is also the statement of Wladimir Dubovec, a former Captain in the
Vlasov Army and now residing in New Jersey: "Ivan [John] Demjanjuk was a
soldier in the 2nd Division of the Vlasov Army at a time when I was
Commander of a security detail to protect General Trukhin. I declare that an ex-
concentration camp guard absolutely would not be permitted membership in the
Vlasov Army."[75] Dubovec was not asked to testify; we do not know why.

Josef Marszalek, a renowned Polish historian and specialist in the history of
the three death camps in Poland, refused to participate in the Demjanjuk trial
because of the "insulting, farcical and almost incomprehensible invitation" in a
letter dated November 3, 1987 and sent to him by a clerk identified as E.
Ytzchak of the Jerusalem court.

In World War II Eastern Europe, there were "Ivans" all over the place. It
was a handy name or appellation for the Nazis to hang on to these nondescript,

---

73. *The Spotlight,* May 2, 1988
74. This information was related to me by a member of the Demjanjuk defense
team. Even more interesting is that his interview of Franz was captured on a video tape
which could easily have been played in the courtroom.
75. Paraphrased from German magazine, *Bunte,* September, 1988.

bullnecked, round-faced peasants. They were not individuals, only sub-humans or swamp creatures to be used or eliminated from this earth with no great loss. Treblinka had its share of Ivans. It also had its share of Kapos, that is, Jewish inmates in supervisory positions whose job it was to control all the other inmates. Rewards were paid for these services.

Jean-Francois Steiner, in his book *Treblinka,* describes Kapo Rakowski, a giant Polish Jew:

> *It was at evening roll call that Kapo Rakowski officially took commmand of the camp. Over six and a half feet tall and almost a yard wide, with a huge mop of curly black hair and coarse features – that was Rakowski. On the border line between man and monster, he possessed Herculean strength and an insatiable appetite. During the great era of speculation the prisoners had called him the King of Speculation, and the Germans, to whom his prowess had been reported, Oberspekulant.*

Continuing with Steiner's commentary, Rakowski

> *could drink a fifth of vodka without showing the least sign of intoxication....The Germans organized a 'religious' wedding for him, and he was given a small private room for his love nest. . . . Rakowski was incapable of fearing anyone or anything, with the possible exception of hunger. He generally had five meals a day, all washed down with wine and vodka.*[76]

Rakowski was an ideal servant for the Germans, and kapo-overlord of his fellow Jews. Unfortunately for him, he had two mortal enemies, who eventually framed Rakowski by having a bag of gold planted under his bunk, and then informing two S.S. men of his "thievery ." Four guards and two head guards were ordered to take him to the "hospital," with his hands tied behind him. "The impassive colossus towered over the six men who bracketed him. For the first time in Treblinka, perhaps, the killers looked like what they were. . . . It took seven of them to kill a single man, unarmed and bound."[77]

Would it not be a supreme irony if a Polish Jew, and a Kapo at that, was the real Ivan the Terrible of Treblinka?

76. Steiner, op. cit. , p. 243.
77. Ibid., p. 296.

The following blood-curdling description from Steiner's collection of interviews of survivors makes one wonder about the apparently personal and first-hand memory of witness Rosenberg:

Adolf is running toward the gas chambers. He is going to set fire to them. Suddenly, Ivan, the sadistic giant, appears in his path. The Ukrainian seems a little bewildered, surprised, but not frightened. His black eyes stare at Adolf, Adolf's hands, Adolf's belt, looking for a possible weapon. They do not see one. Ivan decides not to draw his revolver. His knees slightly flexed, his hands open, he waits for the little Jew who keeps running toward him. Ivan smiles. He is completely at ease in his skin, in his body rich with blood, flesh and muscle.

He blocks without flinching when Adolf tries to butt him in the stomach. Knotting both hands around Adolf's throat, he lifts him up and lays him on the ground. Lying on Adolf, crushing him with his full weight, he begins to strangle him. He dies in the act. One minute later, when Djielo reaches his friend's body, he will see first the wide back of the Ukrainian, and then the dagger planted in it with Adolf 's hand clutching the handle.

Adolf's dead body is covered by Ivan's, but in his eyes is an expression not usually found on the faces of strangled men. It is as if, at the very moment he died, Adolf felt only the immense joy of knowing that he had finally managed to unsheathe the Ukrainian's dagger and had dealt him a mortal wound.[78]

According to *The Jerusalem Post*, July 4, 1987, Haim Sztajer, seventy-eight, came all the way from Melbourne, Australia to testify. A leader of the uprising, "he met Ivan the Terrible in the camp's yard, picked up a shovel and hit him. The blow did not kill Ivan because, when Sztajer returned to the same spot minutes later, the Ukrainian was gone." Interestingly, he insisted that a "Liudas Kairys" of Chicago was the real Ivan the Terrible. With the help of other prisoners, Sztajer admitted that he "killed other Ukrainian guards, including Ivan's partner Nikolai, with the blade of a large pair of tailor's scissors ."

According to the *Ukrainian Weekly* of March 29, 1987, the Israeli news agency *Itim* reported on March 22, 1987 that a Polish court had convicted three

78. Ibid., *Treblinka*, p. 296

farmers for "perjury" for saying that Ivan the Terrible was killed in the prison uprising of August, 1943. The farmers stated that Ivan frequently drank vodka with them in their homes near the camp. After the uprising, the visits abruptly stopped and they heard that he had been killed. The notorious Jacek Wilczur[79] had a hand in this conviction, and we wonder that an idle statement could cause such consternation and swift retribution against three humble farmers.

We are forced to conclude by asking how many Ivans were killed, and how many times and in how many ways was the real Ivan the Terrible was killed. And why is John Demjanjuk now portrayed as the real Ivan come-to-life?

The Jewish nation is being discredited by the machinations of a handful of evil men, and the Jerusalem lower court has perverted justice into a despicable and tortured word in the Holy Land. That the court's conduct and logic is preposterous and that it defames Israel is of no consequence to them. Erstwhile victims have now become oppressors.

79. see p. 4.

CHAPTER NINE – THE VERDICT AND THE WILD RHETORIC IN THE COURTROOM

Levin's verdict, written in an astonishingly short time after the trial's conclusion, is outrageous, disgraceful and unacceptable. Its 800 pages of disjointed, tortuous rationalizations are a sea of rhetoric aimed at the emotions which serves to perpetrate an outrage against an innocent man. Levin's own statement is revealing:

> *The importance of such a protocol is that it gives the Court and the Defense a reliable picture of the events as they happened at that time, the absence of which may result in a situation that a reliable picture may not be given in front of the Court which has to deal with this matter, and its knowledge may be deprived of hints, struggles and things which emerge from these components, which have the power to contribute and influence the conclusion of the Court.*[80]

The first portion of the verdict recites World War II history in an attempt to establish the framework and frightening atmosphere for the crucifixion of John Demjanjuk. Although unable to blame him for the entire war, the court's goal seems to be to portray Demjanjuk as the vital cog that made one huge death camp work. First, it discusses the disenfranchisement of the Jewish people in Germany, steps that range from isolation to confiscatory measures. This development was decided at the Wannsee Conference on January 20, 1942, a conference that was concerned with the "final solution." After the conquest of Poland, the Nazis created a new entity in that country called the "Government-General." Jews were ghettoized and persecution led to extermination. No mention was made in the verdict of the infamous Molotov-Von Ribbentrop Treaty, the Nazi Germany-Soviet Russia partnership, which had an important bearing on the final solution of the "Jewish problem."

According to the court's exposition of the Jewish experience, individual shooting and bloodshed on a mass scale were "affecting the mental stability of the officers and men of the operational formations,"[81] therefore Himmler and

---

80. Verdict, p. 0497.
81. Verdict, p. 0057.

his S.S. cohorts had to find a quick, clean and efficient way to conduct the mass extermination. Using their experience in their own T-4 euthanasia program wherein they dispatched some 100,000 of their own German defectives and incurables, they chose poison gas as the answer. On September 3, 1941, the first gassing with Zyklon B was done on Soviet prisoners. According to experts, Zyklon B, a commercially manufactured fumigant intended for fleas and lice packed in 200-gram tin cans, was used in the concentration camps for disinfectant purposes. The verdict never addressed the question as to how this chemical was converted into a mechanism for human destruction.

Odilo Globocnik, an Austrian-appointed director of the Reinhardt Operation to exterminate European Jewry, (and to whom Karl Streible, head of Trawniki, was subordinate), was provided with ninety-two "specialists" from ten to twelve T-4 centers in Germany, who were ordered to conduct mass killings in Belzec, Sobibor and Treblinka. Some 5,000 guards and watchmen were processed and trained at the Trawniki training camp near Lublin, consisting primarily of *Volksdeutschen* (ethnic Germans), Ukrainians and Baltic POWs, the latter two groups referred to as *Hiwis,* short for *Hilfswillige,* or volunteer helpers. It is estimated that twenty to thirty Germans were assigned to each camp along with some 120 recruited Soviet POWs.

According to the lower court, Christian Wurth (aka Wirth), Commander of Camp Belzec, used carbon monoxide gas from a diesel motor to kill his victims. However, according to the U.S. Environmental Protection Agency, diesel gas actually helps prevent suffocation since it contains 16 to 18% oxygen compared to the 21% already in the atmosphere. The government reports that diesel-powered motors emit only trace amounts of carbon monoxide; instead of hydrocarbons, diesels emit particulate matter in the form of soot or smoke. Subsequently, the court itself unwittingly codified a very serious question about the function of a diesel engine capable of serving as an instrument for mass-killing, and it is a profound one in that it raises questions about the extent of the Holocaust. American, German and Polish experts now seriously question the accuracy of the enormous numbers of victims of the Holocaust.

Since the camp commanders could not keep up with the pace of the human cargo, a new gas house was erected, containing ten chambers and operated in the same manner. A German S.S. man named Fritz Schmidt was in charge of the motor room where the gas was produced, and he was periodically relieved by men identified only as Munzberger and Matthes, and other Germans. One must wonder when Ivan and his alleged assistant, Nikolai, who supposedly perished during the uprising, had their turn operating the diesel motor. The Germans and Ukrainians were unable to peer through a window of the chamber to verify when all occupants were dead because of the bluish smoke from the diesel motor.

In describing the exit of those still alive from the freight cars to the platform of the Treblinka railway station and hence to the path of death into the gas chamber, Levin says: "This was the horror, this was the terror and this was the flutter of the wings of death which hovered over all those arriving at the Treblinka extermination camp." Furthermore, he borrows commentary from Yitzak Arad, director of the Yad Vashem Memorial Museum: "After the descent from the freight cars, the devils' dance began, a wicked roundabout of violence and slaughter, obscuring feelings and blind obedience to the commands of the Germans and their Ukrainian minions."[82] The use of such dramatic and theatrical language could only be meant to appeal to the emotions.

The recitation of procedures at Treblinka includes identification of the railroad station which could accommodate up to twenty coaches or freight cars, the waiting guards who would whip and drive the unfortunates to the undressing yard, and the women later to a barbershop where their hair was shorn for Third Reich use; and then to the *Schlauch*, the 100-meter *himmelstrasse*, or "road to heaven." It was 2 1/2 meters wide with the sides made of barbed wire and concealed by intertwined tree branches. At the barbershop, the women were attended by fifteen barbers trained to shear heads in five quick scissor strokes. Since the frightened women did not want to enter the shop, Ivan forced them inside with a bayonet. "They were wounded and whole pieces of flesh were hanging down from their backs and they were bleeding profusely."[83] There must have been as much blood and gore on the barbershop floor as in the *Schlauch*, especially when hundreds of thousands of people were involved.

In addition to collecting the shorn womens' hair for industrial use in Germany, Treblinka had a crew of victims called "dentists." As the dead bodies were being carted from the gas chambers to the burial pits on the run by stretcher bearers, it was the function of a line of these "dentists" to rapidly extract false teeth containing gold from the corpses. Sometimes diamonds were found concealed in the crowns of the teeth. One must wonder at the extreme

82. Verdict, p. 0116-117
83. Verdict, p. 0141.

skill of the "dentists" to attend to their work while running alongside the stretcher bearers; and, if there were a line of six, how did they avoid getting in each other's way?

Then there is a description of the role of a group of Jewish forced laborers known as "gravediggers," who would receive the corpses thrown into the pits by the stretcher bearers, arrange them layer by layer, the face of one next to the feet of another to increase the capacity of the pits. The gravediggers must have been of Herculean strength and energy to keep pace with the output of the gas chambers; and the pits must have been awfully deep, especially one containing 200,000 corpses. The verdict also relates that a sticky, pink, bubbling substance arose from the corpses but the chemistry for this phenomenon was not understood.

The verdict then discusses the German necessity to hide the evidence of the crime by digging up and burning the corpses because "In the spring of 1942 . . . the German forces began retreating."[84] For a precise and thoroughly researched exposition of World War II history, this is still another misstatement that reflects badly on the lower court. The change in fortune for the German army is generally accepted as the Battle of Stalingrad which began on July 17, 1942 and ended on February 2, 1943.

The deceased — indeed if he ever did exist — Ignat Trantiwitz Danilchenko of Tobolsk, Russia, suddenly and mysteriously surfaced late in the trial. Apparently, it seemed to be good public relations to create a "comrade" — Danilchenko — for Demjanjuk, one who had also collaborated with the Germans, who had also been a KZ guard, and who had helped commit atrocities in the Sobibor concentration camp. But there are glaring weaknesses in this attempt to contrive evidence. In the same way that Russia fed false information to *The Soviet Way* and *News From Ukraine,* its mouthpieces in New York City, it was a Russian-language newspaper in Israel, *Nasha Strana,* that was the source for this story, an amazing "revelation" in that it did not surface for more than forty years. There are many abnormalities in the story, including a so-called corroborating document which was produced in *News From Ukraine,* and much discussion regarding the original Soviet source of the documentation, especially that country's consummate skill "in acts of forgery and inducing mistakes and fabricating evidence,[85] the most notorious "falsifier" being Procurator Roman Rudenko. John Demjanjuk was described by Danilchenko as wearing an S.S. uniform at Sobibor, but this was impossible because only German guards wore S.S. uniforms with the S.S. insignia. And again, the all-

84. Verdict, p. 0166
85. Verdict, p. 0509.

important question: How does one cross-examine a dead man, if a Danilchenko really existed?

Judge Levin attempts to partially resolve this quandary by stating that "the mass extermination activities in Treblinka in which about 870,000 Jews were annihilated, began in July 1942 and terminated at the end of January 1943."[86] At that point, Demjanjuk was transferred to Sobibor, where he continued his evil work. But this contradicts all the witnesses' assertions that the mass Treblinka killings went on until the uprising of August 2, 1943, and continued even through September, and that Demjanjuk was an intrinsic part of that slaughter. Also, if the real Ivan was assaulted and killed during the uprising in Treblinka, he could not possibly have been at Sobibor.

Levin also makes another contradictory claim in that when Treblinka was in a state of liquidation after March 1943, Ivan was active in "the transfer of the remaining Jews for extermination at Sobibor," and definitively declares that "it was proved that the remnants of the Jews who remained in Treblinka were in fact sent to Sobibor and exterminated in their mechanisms."[87] How is it then that some 600 Jews remained in Treblinka to participate in the uprising? Even more noteworthy is the assertion of Treblinka expert Jean-Francois Steiner, that a *thousand* Jews were in Treblinka[88] in August, 1943.

The judge also curiously alludes to a possibility that "there were two Ukrainian Ivans incredibly resembling each other, the one Ivan Grozni, who was active at Treblinka, and the other Ivan Dejmanjuk [Demjanjuk] , who was active at Sobibor, but this is an extremely unlikely occurrence . . . " He emphasizes his statement by declaring, "It has to be extremely coincidental and out of the ordinary, for such a thing to happen."[89] Yet, why is a possible mistake in identification beyond the realm of probability, especially when the Germans referred to all Ukrainians and Russians as "Ivan"?

Levin, moreover, discredits a list provided by the World Jewish Congress on July 6, 1976 of twenty Treblinka survivors who were unable to identify John Demjanjuk contending that: "This list cannot tell us anything. And their inability to identify is of no value . . . . [This list] is not able to contribute anything whatsoever to the undermining of the identification which was established by the other survivors."[90]

In the verdict, Levin also reiterated some of Rosenberg's testimony, oblivious of his sworn admission that he and a certain Gustav collaborated in

86. Verdict, p. 0516.
87. Verdict, p. 0518.
88. *Treblinka,* Jean-Francois Steiner, p. 303.
89. Verdict, p. 0518.
90. Verdict, p. 0526-7.

the killing of Ivan and left him "lying there for all eternity." Levin readily accepted Rosenberg's adjusted explanation that Ivan's death was only a rumor that he heard in the forest, and which was due to wishful thinking. A neutral observer would note that 1947 is closer to 1943 than is 1988, and Rosenberg's memory might have been much better in 1947, especially when he chose to submit a sworn statement which he signed on each of eight pages.

Levin also reiterates that Epstein was allegedly in close proximity to Ivan for an "extended" period. Epstein described Ivan as

> *a man of vast proportions, well built, solid, and he was operating the motor, he was performing some action and pressing on something which activated the motor. After that, we would wait for twenty minutes to half an hour, and then they ordered the doors to be opened, these were very wide doors, and the corpses to be taken out. Ivan would come out of this room and would rain murderous blows on us with the pipe. Sometimes, he would come with a dagger, sometimes with a bayonet, and he would crack skulls, he would cut off ears, he would brutalize the prisoners, it is absolutely unbelievable, unbelievable, and he would stand next to the corpses and gaze upon them. . . it was horrible to look at the corpses when they took them out of the cabins.*
>
> *People with crushed faces, people with stab wounds, pregnant women with stab wounds in their bellies, women with the fetus hanging half out, young girls with stab wounds on their breasts, with eyes gouged out. I find it difficult to portray this scene.* [91]

Though Demjanjuk's build can hardly be described as being of "vast proportions," it is a cause of wonderment that such inflammatory rhetoric was used repeatedly, without restraint, all directed toward Demjanjuk. And yet, the witnesses who identified the real Ivan as a giant of a man somehow were not called to testify.

Compounding the demagoguery, it was Levin's nauseating practice, illegal in most civilized countries, to wax eloquently over the prosecution witnesses themselves. For example, he described witness Cherney as being

> *a sensitive person, and an honest man, with an aptitude for expressing himself, who has managed to recall from his enduring memory what he*

had experienced, he and the other deportees to extermination, during the difficult and terror-stricken time within the freight cars.

It would seem that there is no more faithful, reliable and shocking description than this one which emerged from Cherney's testimony. What writer or producer could write an account of the experience clearer and more biting than that voiced by Cherney with a broken heart and tearful eyes in the court in Israel?[92]

The witness also stated, "I remember that people went mad, absolutely mad. They began to drink urine." One must ask, where did the supply of urine come from in the packed cattle cars? The outlandish declaration was obviously intended to contribute shock value to the trial. Such rhetoric indicates extreme prejudice and use of sensationalism, and is further evidence that Levin's decision had already been reached.

Levin also reviews the testimony of witnesses whom he refers to by number:

Witness 153 recognized a Ukrainian guard called Ivan Grozni, Grozni being the Polish word for "the terrible." The witness "used to see him going across the camp almost every day. He was, according to him, nearly always drunk. He carried a whip and bayonet and whipped the prisoners[93] But when shown the pictures of Demjanjuk and Fedorenko, he could not identify either man.

Witness 154 was in Treblinka from the camp's establishment to his escape during the uprising. He could not identify a single picture of Demjanjuk, but could identify the picture of one Ukrainian who limped heavily. However, this testimony was dismissed since "he had no close knowledge of the Ukrainians at Treblinka. He did not know Ivan the Terrible. He did not hear of his exploits, did not see him, and it is not surprising that he did not identify him but it would seem that his capacity to identify or the level of the information he accrued are defective since he attributed the picture of the Ukrainian Fedorenko from Treblinka to a German S.S. man."[94]

Witness 155 was also at Treblinka during the full time of its operation, and his testimony was just as vacuous. Witness 156, another full-timer and who worked in the laundry recalled a Ukrainian guard named Ivan Grozni, describing him as 5 feet 5 inches, hardly a giant; but he could not recall any marks or facial characteristics. The best that witness 158 could do was to say

92. Verdict, 0112.
93. Verdict, 0532.
94. Verdict, p. 0535

that John Demjanjuk "looked like a Ukrainian guard at Treblinka." He had not personally met this guard who roamed all over the two camps, but had heard from other inmates that he was a murderer. Witness 166 recalled the name of a Ukrainian guard called Ivan, but did not know him personally; he had only heard about him.[95]

Witness 167, another full-timer, stated that there were five German guards and about 250 Ukrainian guards. He had heard the name Ivan Grozni but was "not certain that he ever saw him and was unable to make a connection between him and the pictures that were shown to him."[96] The reality is that there were far fewer guards in number. The interviewee was unable to give any particulars with respect to the subject of identification of Ivan or Fedorenko — neither their names, their nationality, their uniforms nor any other identifying marks. Witnesses 157 and 160-165 were at Treblinka for only short periods: 157 for eleven days; 160 for one month; 161 for four days; 162 for one day; 163 for one day; and 164 for four hours. Although witness 165 was in Treblinka for only three weeks, he identified Ivan as "a person in his thirties, of height 5.7 feet, with a fat build and dark brown hair."[97] After seemingly demolishing the twenty witnesses, several of whom are unlisted for unknown reasons, Judge Levin mentions one Alfred Billitz, a subject located in a UN file, and whom the Defense asserted was the real Ivan the Terrible. But Levin declared: "What is clear and obvious from all the evidence is that Ivan Grozni is of Ukrainian extraction whereas Alfred Bilitz [sic], who indeed was present in Treblinka, was of German extraction. . . ."[98] His conclusion was that there was no connection between him and Ivan, operator of the gas chambers.

Then suddenly, Judge Dov Levin announces the astounding and unbelievable decision that,

THE ACCUSED, IVAN JOHN DEJMANJUK [DEMJANJUK] – IS IVAN GROZNI OF TREBLINKA

Having arrived at the conclusion of the chapter on identification in this case, which can be defined as the very heart of this case, and the basis for our decision, we guide ourselves according to the basic principles detailed below, the values of which we will keep closely in mind.

95. Verdict, p. 0537
96. Verdict, p. 0543
97. Verdict, p. 0540
98. Verdict, p. 0552

(a) In laying down our findings as regards the facts, we have to be convinced that they have been proven in front of us beyond all reasonable doubt.

(b) That a decision on a matter of identification of a person, on the basis of identifying eye witnesses, requires strict and cautious examination of the evidence, lest, Heaven forbid, the Court should fail by making findings based on a mistaken identity, either deliberately or by mistake, an identification which is based on an amazing likeness between the accused and Ivan Grozni of Treblinka.

(c) The uniqueness of the case in consideration, which we dealt with in Chapter 65 above, and our impression of the power of the memory of events and images of Treblinka, in the consciousness of the identifying witnesses which we dealt with in Chapters 65 – 66 above.

(d) The ability of human beings to remember images and identify them, with the certainty required, also after many years, even after fort y years, especially in the very very distinctive and exceptional circumstances, as described above.

(e) The law which applies in Israel regarding evidence of identity and identity parades, as interpreted from time to time, and as it is desirable to apply them in the special circumstances of this case.

What we have done, therefore, and after we have considered and examined strictly all the evidence on this subject, responsibly and with the full caution required, we have determined decisively, and without any hesitation or doubt, that the accused Ivan John Demjanjuk, who stands on trial before us, is Ivan who is established as Ivan Grozni, the operator of the gas chambers at Treblinka, and the executor of the cruel and sadistic deeds which have been described above:

(a) It is sufficient for us to come to the above conclusion, on the accumulated strength, and on a consideration of all the elements of identification, which have crystallized and converged, layer upon layer, link upon link, in the statements taken by Mrs. Radivker within the framework of her investigation, and the first statement of Epstein

taken by the investigator Koler [Koller] We obviously add to this, strengthening the general dependability and reliability of the identification, the stable and impressive evidence of the witnesses examined by them, namely, Rosenberg, Tzirni [Cherney] , Burekas [Boraks] and Epstein.

(b) To the decisive force of the above mentioned evidence and statements, which stand on their own, we join the strength and serious and independent weight of the identity parades, in which a set of pictures was shown to the witnesses, including the Travniki picture, or the picture which was attributed to the accused and proved, as has been explained above, and as will be explained further below, as a picture of the accused. We are referring to the identification of the accused in these identity parades, by the witnesses Rosenberg, Epstein and Reichman, in distinction from Otto Horn – as explained above.

Each one of the identifications, on the basis of this set of pictures, was perhaps not sufficient to make a definite finding on the strength of such identification only. But the cumulative weight of these identifications creates a completeness, that can be relied on with certainty in making a criminal finding. In these identification there is certainly assistance in a substantial form to the other identifications which we have already dealt with in the previous paragraph. [99]

In other words, one lie will not hold up; but when you pile up one after another until you have an impressive stack of lies, then, magically, the truth will be revealed.

This writer will never forget two things about the "trial of the century" in the Holy Land: the needless violence and barbarity practiced on John Demjanjuk by three "civilized" nations, including my own, and the revealing and shocking admission of Police Inspector-General David Kraus, Israel's top police official: "On occasion, the memories of potential witnesses have to be refreshed."[100]

---

99. Verdict, p. 0552-0555
100. *Jerusalem Post* daily edition, July 30, 1986

CHAPTER TEN – MISCONDUCT OF THE COURT

Attempting to summarize the sordid trial of John Demjanjuk, we have proceeded from a collection of irrefutable facts to tantalizing speculation. The final element is the unknown ending of the story of the aging, tormented American, John Demjanjuk.

In one of many challenges to the court, the eloquent Appeal[101] states:

14A. *Considering the extent of the case, about 10,500 pages of the Record and about 5,000 pages of Exhibits (some in foreign languages without a Hebrew translation), the verdict of the Honorable Lower Court, was written in less than two months, excessive agility, which appears to have, in combination with other factors which were mentioned above, harmed the ability for thorough consideration and meticulous examination of the many and varied items of evidence which were before the Honorable Lower Court.*

B *This excessive speed in handing down the verdict brought about mistakes and erroneous expressions of the Honorable Lower Court, even in subjects which were not in dispute.[102]*

101. The English version of the Demjanjuk Appeal reads: In the Supreme Court Sitting as the Court of Criminal Appeals in Jerusalem. Criminal Appeal/88 *The Appellant:* John (Ivan) Demjanjuk represented by Atty. Y. Sheftel and/or P. Chumak of 2 Levontin St. Tel-Aviv 65111 versus *The Respondent:* State of Israel. The "Notice of Appeal" reads: An Appeal is filed hereby against the verdict of the Jerusalem District Court, sitting as a Special Court, in Criminal Claim 373/86, given on the 8th day of Iyar 5748 (25.4.88), according to which the Appellant was convicted of offenses of crimes against the Jewish People, crimes against humanity, war crimes, crimes against persecuted people, all offenses being according to Paragraph 1 of the Nazi and Nazi Collaborators (Punishment) Law 5710-1950. The sentence pronounced on the Appellant in respect of the above mentioned offenses is death.

The Appeal is lodged against the conviction of the Appellant on each of the offenses of which he was convicted and alternatively against the severity of the sentence pronounced by the Honorable Lower Court.

102. Demjanjuk Appeal (henceforth referred to as Appeal), p. 27.

If it thus erred so wrongly in that direction, how much more so in the facts that were disputed?

In the blistering Appeal, the Defense refers to the "honorable" lower court's insulting and injurious comments while displaying obvious disdain toward the defense. Attention is called to the court's intimidation and excessive intervention of Defense witnesses, and its agreeable acceptance of the testimony of brazenly false witnesses, completely ignoring contradictory evidence that would have benefited the defendant A prime example was the acceptance of a story of a man "who was in two different places at the same time." Shouts of contempt and unmentionably foul language along with threats of bodily harm issued from the audience toward the Defense. This incredible conduct occurred throughout the course of the hearings, and more so during the recess.

The court did not restrain or halt the prosecution witnesses' exaggerations of the Treblinka persecutions It refused to admit exhibits into evidence even when they met the standards of admissibility. A lesson in the history and horrors of the Holocaust was given precedence over the guilt or innocence of John Demjanjuk, a departure from all proper procedures of criminal law since it psychologically and emotionally overpowers the rights of the individual.

The great British jurist Thomas Lord Denning, one of the most respected of the twentieth century, was so outraged and provoked by the conduct of this court that he was compelled to voice strenuous objections in a highly regarded British newspaper with a pro-Jewish tradition, the *Daily Telegraph,* declaring: "All that was stated above, without entering into details of the factual and judicial determinations of the Honorable Lower Court, suffices to disqualify and invalidate the entire proceedings and bring about the full exoneration of the Appellant."[103]

Jurisdiction of an Israeli court to judge a person extradited to Israel is derived from and limited by the Warrant of Extradition. The Charge Sheet submitted against the defendant and the clauses of law under which he was convicted deviate from the Warrant of Extradition. John Demjanjuk's trial was conducted, therefore, without the lower court having jurisdiction to try him and therefore the Verdict, Sentence and all factual and judicial findings that were determined are invalid.

The Levin court exposed itself each and every day to "methodical and intentional incitement"[104] in the print media by contracting with Yif'at Ltd, a clipping service, to receive clippings from the eight major daily newspapers, but refused to order the service to present an album of these clippings to the

---

103. Appeal, p. 30.
104. Appeal, p. 1.

Defense, again frustrating the defendant from receiving due justice. It also held frequent " judicial" meetings with reporters who, thus encouraged, created "wild incitement" against John Demjanjuk , his counsel and the Ukrainian people, and despite the request by Demjanjuk's counsel, the court refused to appeal to the media to cease transgressing the law in their reporting.

The court permitted hordes of press people to be present in the courtroom, which disrupted proceedings, caused undue excitement and intensified hostility toward the defendant and his counsel. This irreparably damaged orderly judicial process. We were pleased to note the comment of the Honorable Judge Haim Cohn, predecessor of the present chief judge, before the trial began: "The conduct of a trial in the midst of public and communications hysteria could create unbearable pressure on the court, frustrate justice being done and *prevent a verdict of not guilty,* even if reality so dictates"[105] (emphasis is in the original).

The lower court made a serious mistake in not stopping the trial when it became clear that institutions such as the Polish High Commission for Investigating Nazi Crimes and the OSI refused to submit evidence that could have helped to prove the innocence of John Demjanjuk or, at least, have contested the Prosecution's evidence. This error is particularly conspicuous by the fact that the doors of these institutions were open, without limitation, to the Prosecution. This act cruelly violated the promise of the State Attorney that, should it be necessary, the Defense team would be permitted to investigate every archive in all corners of the world to obtain needed evidence.

When arrangements were made for the start of the trial, the Defense was given less than one third of the time accorded to the Prosecution, a severe and unethical handicap. The heavy-handed lower court disqualified many Defense questions without there being, in many cases, any objection whatsoever by the Prosecution. This lends credence to the belief that in Israel, you are guilty until you prove yourself innocent.

A grotesque and perverse act was committed by the court in imposing "sanctions" on the Defense, i.e., forbidding Israeli counsel to object to questions by the Prosecution in cross-examination which he did not question in direct examination unless another Defense counsel apologized for a certain remark.

The court was guilty of insulting and extremely crude comments, especially to the Defense's request to release the defendant. The chief judge forbade any criticism on the part of the Defense regarding his judicial practices.

Adding to the insufferable atmosphere, ministers, Knesset members and holders of senior government offices helped to contribute to a lynch-mob

105. Appeal, p. 14.

atmosphere. One minister named Avraham Sharir, holding dual offices in Justice and Tourism, publicly expressed his hope that Demjanjuk would receive the death penalty before sentencing took place.[106]

The Israeli judicial system has an ethereal concept known as the "beginning of admission." It cannot be compared to the beginning of pregnancy, the outcome of which can occasionally be in doubt, especially when wishful thinking is involved. During the constant grilling of John Demjanjuk in his cell, he once uttered a comment: "You are pushing me to Treblinka." Why would he not react in such a manner when all that he heard, over and over, was the word Treblinka? Yet, the police interrogators pounced on this expression, fed it to the judge and, lo and behold, we have the "beginning of admission."

Very upsetting to the police interrogators were John's general expressions to the effect that collaborators with the Nazis were only little cogs in the extermination machine which was constructed and operated by the Germans. And they, the helpers and collaborators, including many Jewish Kapos, by force had no choice whatsoever to refuse the orders issued to them by the Germans Demjanjuk illustrated this point in general terms by declaring to a police plant, Rav Paked a.k.a. Aryeh Kaplan, whom he thought to be a friend, that "the conditions in the prisoner-of-war camps were inhuman, when a German would appear, a Kapo would immediately order to remove hats and the people stood and were afraid to move. If the German didn't like something about someone, he would shoot him on the spot."[107] Judge Levin adroitly interpreted Demjanjuk's[107] comments as an "emotional need to justify himself" for criminal acts, and also saw these statements as the "beginning of admission."

Levin also remarkably infers a conclusion that if it had not been for his qualifying statements, Demjanjuk's words would have been quite a clear confession of criminal activities on his part. This imperious approach really indicates the judge's desire to convict. In still another reprehensible misstatement, Levin defines Demjanjuk as "a person who indirectly opened a window through which can be seen incriminating behavior on his part."[108] Such grasping at straws is unacceptable.

Throughout the trial, gross and shocking misstatements tantalized the neutral observer as, for example, historian Matityahu Maizel's incredible statement that Germany and Poland were allies during World War II. Testifying for the Prosecution, Maizel also claimed that 5.3 million out of 5.5 or 5.7 million displaced persons returned to Russia willingly. It is not known where

---

106. Appeal, p. 6-7
107. Verdict, p. 0760-1.
108. Verdict, p. 0762.

he secured such gross figures because in my own experience with the United States Displaced Persons Commission, Soviet refugees were terrified of the possibility of voluntary or forcible return to the USSR. It was also stated that enforced repatriation to Russia was stopped in the American occupied zone of Germany at the end of 1945. But, I saw with my own eyes the feared Russian repatriation teams driving around the American Zone, with hammer-and-sickle flags on their vehicles, as late as the end of 1950.

In addition to this trial being a repository of lies, ridiculous exaggerations and wild innuendos, we marvel at the skillful use Israel has made of cohorts in other countries. We have already discussed the matter of the OSI's withholding of exculpatory evidence and the close cooperation of Jacek Wilczur of the Polish Communist government. During the closing weeks of the Demjanjuk trial, we were astonished to learn that now Italy had issued a warrant for Demjanjuk's arrest for the usual atrocities and killings, a popular charge that is so easily bandied about. We wrote for clarification to the appropriate court in Trieste and, as expected, received no reply.

Doing some basic research we read allegations that in 1943, the notorious Odilo Globocnik and fifty S.S. men were sent to northern Italy and ordered to build a KZ camp at San Sabbo near Trieste to exterminate Italian Jews, Communists and partisans However, one authority disputes this, saying that their real assignment was to protect a vital military zone against Yugoslav and Italian partisans. Whatever the case, in addition to the S.S. men, Globocnik used mainly Italians as his helpers. This story was developed by a Communist Yugoslav magazine which accused John Demjanjuk of being part of Globocnik's staff and murdering thousands of Jews, partisans and anti-fascists.[109]

In reality, Germans ran the camp, the guards were mostly Italian, and there never was a mass killing camp in Italy. Some 150 witnesses gave depositions at the Trieste criminal trial in 1975-76. Not one mentioned John Demjanjuk or an Ivan the Terrible. All of the so-called collaborators were granted amnesty — hardly a punishment for grave crimes, and a poor reflection on the efficiency of Israel's confederates in Italy.

Attempting to follow through on the brand-new charge against Demjanjuk, a close associate telephoned an attorney and friend in Trieste for details. The lawyer told him that the charge was "nonsense." We can only conclude that this is still another diversionary tactic to keep the Demjanjuk pot boiling. However,

---

109. Hans-Peter Rullman, *Victim Of The Holocaust* (Hamburg, Germany. Publisher: Hans-Peter Rullman, 1987) p. 71. His reference is to the Yugoslav news magazine *NIN* (Belgrade).

this would appear to be a bonanza for the Defense since it places John Demjanjuk in three different places at the same time.

It is our feeling that we have painted a comprehensive picture of the John Demjanjuk case. Selected arbitrarily as the man who committed at first hand the most heinous crimes in history, we have followed the tortuous path that he has taken.

Once an American citizen living in a sedate Cleveland suburb, he was unceremoniously denounced as "Nazi No. 1" and yanked from obscurity to being named the world's greatest anti-hero by yellow-dog journalists. A three-nation conspiracy was quickly organized and the hapless man shipped to an isolation cell in the steamy city of Jerusalem. Aside from his misery and privations, we viewed a farcical trial where a contrived identity card was to be the principal evidence against him. When the preposterous card was literally laughed out of the courtroom, the so-called judges decided to rely on the 44-year old memories of several disturbed "witness-survivors" to justify a verdict of guilt. No matter that their star witness was guilty of many lies and deception, and that far more survivors who were unable to identify John were not permitted to testify. To the eternal shame of the three "judges," they pandered to the hunger of the psychopathic zealots who crave for a symbol of the Holocaust, innocent or not, on whom they could wreak their vengeance. Shockingly, even their prime minister became part of the mob crying out for blood.

The sad part of this story is not so much the bitter fate of John Demjanjuk, but the revelation that one cannot get a fair trial in Israel; that Israel itself has downgraded the true picture of the Holocaust; that Israel has deadly tentacles that reach into other countries; that the good Jews of Israel are shamed by evil leaders; and that the real victims of the Holocaust will not find rest as a result.

CHAPTER ELEVEN – CONCLUSION – OR IS IT?

We leave the John Demjanjuk case as we found it — a tangled puzzle with a hapless human being used as a defenseless pawn by deceitful, unconscionable conspirators. The case — a bland word when it pertains to a human life — is complex, bewildering, and has endless trails that lead nowhere. It does leave fascinating questions, however. Why was it necessary for three countries of inestimable wealth and power to unite and concentrate their resources on the persecution of a country boy of misty origin?

The United States, sad to say, played the most shameful role in this scenario. It, after all, literally declared war on one of its own citizens of thirty-five years standing. It made a rag of its supposedly protective Constitution and made our Statue of Liberty, symbol of succor and sanctuary, weep. It literally forced the State of Israel to be a partner in the crime of destroying an American.

Israel, for its part, played an equally repugnant role. One can only cringe at John Demjanjuk's mistreatment — from the moment of his arrival when he was forbidden to kiss the soil of the "holy" land, to his brutal interrogations, to the wild rides from prison to court, when he was dreadfully injured (with full knowledge of the "judges") — one befitting perhaps only a ferocious or deadly animal. Equally garish was the pretext of a foreordained verdict where huzzahs and cheers greeted the Prosecution and derision and scorn were offered to the Defense. The humiliation of the world-renowned Count Tolstoy is a case in point. And, one can never forget the obscene jubilation and rejoicing of the select audience at the grisly verdict, and the ugly, active participation at the trial of none less than the Prime Minister himself.

And, all the time, the third partner of the triumvirate, Russia, smugly watched Israel do its dirty work. Russia — which should have been charged with war crimes at Nuremberg for the Katyn Forest massacre, the slaughter at Vinnytsia, and the horrible mass murder of its own Soviet citizens during the postwar repatriations — played a quiet, "saintly" role as might be expected of a cold-blooded killer. And, we do not even discuss Russia's orchestration of the horrendous man-made famine that took upwards of seven million Ukrainian victims during 1932-33, a true war of genocide against helpless Ukraine.

What was the motivation of the fiendishly clever Russians in concocting the brew that embroiled Demjanjuk in a maelstrom of madness? Was the purpose to strike terror in the hearts of all Ukrainians living abroad so that they would not reveal the true nature of the Soviet beast? Or, was there a simple and cordial agreement to release hundreds of thousands of Jewish refuseniks, which Israel desperately needs for demographic reasons, in a pitiless exchange whereby Israel will show its gratitude by acting as a commercial executioner? Or, maybe we are seeing the foundation of an ambitious genocide program for the deportation and trial of American servicemen in former enemy countries?

Only time will tell. And if there is any justice left in the world, the moles and real war criminals who permeate the sanctuaries of the above mentioned governments will some day have to come out into the sunshine and be exposed.

As we reflect on the component parts of the John Demjanjuk case, we are overwhelmed by its illegal, unethical and cruel aspects. We recall that its basis was the monstrous OSI created at enormous expense to the American taxpayer — not to combat the present-day menace of Communism and its vile and cunning agents such as Jonathan Pollard — but to resuscitate "Nazi" ghosts of half a century ago. Its most urgent need is for targets. We remember the key role played by ex-Congresswoman Elizabeth Holtzman and one wonders if monetary donations influence our Congress and other branches of the U.S. government to obey the edicts of the Holtzman-OSI actions. What inspired the manipulative OSI to change the tenor of this case from "traitor to the Motherland" to that of Jew-killer of almost one million Jews? We wonder at the unbelievable passivity of our Congress when it ignores the blatant culpability of the OSI in withholding exculpatory evidence.

And of course we must understand the role of the "little foxes," such as the editor of *News From Ukraine*. Who provided the idea and the defective materials to him for the article that commenced this tragedy, and who provided the collaboration that was essential to point the finger at Demjanjuk? Why was this editor not the subject of a lawsuit for his libelous and ridiculous accusations?

So we are left with a list of pertinent questions for the reader to contemplate, in the hope that it may inspire some powerful and just official or officials to overturn the travesty that occurred in Israel:

1. Did John Demjanjuk receive fair treatment in the U.S. judicial system?

2. Was the intent of the U.S. Constitution violated?

3. Was Frank Battisti a fit judge to oversee the first trial of John

Demjanjuk? If not, why was he not removed from this particular case, especially when he himself was under a Federal Grand Jury investigation?

4. When ten judges rebelled against his conduct, why was Battisti not removed for cause?

5. Why was the U.S. Marshals department not punished for its uncalled-for activity in this case?

6. Who called the signals for the preposterous conduct of the Israeli court that broke every single rule of judicial conduct and comportment?

7. Why did the Israeli prime minister, himself a former terrorist and possible war criminal, interject himself as a participant in the trial by virtue of congratulating the prosecution witnesses in the courtroom during the ongoing trial? Did he not intimidate the entire judicial process?

8. Why were the three Polish witnesses who could have cleared John Demjanjuk beyond the shadow of a doubt stopped from leaving Poland to testify?

9. Since Eliyahu Rosenberg, the star witness for the prosecution, was so utterly discredited with his many and conflicting stories, why did not this fact alone collapse the trial?

10. In view of all the sage observations and conclusions made by impartial and real judicial experts such as Lord Denning and Judge Haim Cohn, why were their conclusions and recommendations ignored?

11. Regarding the painting of "Ivan the Terrible" that hangs in the Yad Vashem Museum in Jerusalem, is he the real Ivan? If so, he bears no resemblance to John Demjanjuk whatsoever.

12. What has Israel gained and what does it expect to gain in the future as the result of this monstrous case of persecution?

EPILOGUE

A recent photograph of John Demjanjuk shows his face to be almost unrecognizable. There are deep furrows in his brow, and the unending incarceration is evidently taking its toll on the mind and body of this innocent man.

On September 8, 1988, Dov Eitan, the youngest retired judge in Israeli history, was retained as a third lawyer on the Defense team. Shortly thereafter, Eitan announced that he was appalled by the conduct of the three-judge panel that heard the Demjanjuk case and, after consulting with John in Ayalon prison, declared his belief that Demjanjuk was an innocent man. This may have been a mistake, for on November 29, 1988, Dov Eitan dropped from the fifteenth-floor window of a Jerusalem building. This incident is extremely suspicious in that shoe polish was found on the window sill, polish that would have to come from the top and sides of his shoes. We have also heard that his suit contained no identification, and that he had an appointment to meet his wife later that morning.

The day before this dreadful event, the highly intelligent Eitan had been in a happy and cheerful mood. He had already established a warm and cordial relationship with Demjanjuk and looked with relish toward the challenge of freeing him. Lead attorney Sheftel had already agreed to entrust Eitan with a major portion of the Defense efforts. In a letter to the editor of the *Jerusalem Post,* a close friend of Eitan's described him as "a person of wit, charm and elegance. He had a powerful sense of public responsibility and enjoyed moral authority rare in anyone anywhere . . . in 1976, he had joined the Israeli judiciary, expressing pride in his public responsibilities." This hardly describes a man who would take his own life, which is what the Israeli police immediately declared his death to be — a suicide.

As if this were not enough, Yoram Sheftel had acid thrown in his face while attending Eitan's funeral; his left eye was badly injured. The only favorable result of these two catastrophes is that John Demjanjuk's appeal was adjourned to May, 1990, if indeed that can be called favorable.

These two events portend an ominous future. What first-rate lawyer will now be willing to enter a case where the spectre of violence is always present or, at the very least, risk a ruined legal career in an atmosphere of extreme prejudice? Will the archives of the world now be opened to the Demjanjuk

Defense just as they were so conveniently opened for the Prosecution? Will decent Israelis, who so often expressed disgust and revulsion at the conduct of the trial judges, now deluge their government and media with demands for justice and fair play for John Demjanjuk?

For the rest of us, so-called humanity, can we continue to acquiesce passively to the torture of the mind and flesh of an innocent man who rots in a lonely cell? The good God who has blessed us with free will must weep when He gazes down on the smiling man with the beautiful singing voice. What toll will He wreak upon us for our cruelty and stupidity?

Mr. Chaim Herzog is the President of Israel. He is a man of reason, honor , integrity and compassion. It is this writer's understanding that President Herzog has the power to exonerate John Demjanjuk. It is my hope that the people of the world will take pen in hand and appeal to this good man for the immediate release of the innocent victim of the three-nation conspiracy.

Please write to:

Honorable Chaim Herzog
President, State of Israel
Jerusalem, Israel